All Parishioners Great and Small

The Adventures of a Small-Town, Small-Time Pastor*

Eddie Brown

*All Parishioners Great and Small:
The Adventures of a Small-Town, Small-Time Pastor
in Rural America at the End of the Twentieth and
the Beginning of the Twenty-First Centuries,
Anno Domini MMXXII.

*To my partner in life and ministry,
an unconventional pastor's wife—Wes.*

Contents

A Word from the Author 1

Preface 3

1 "From Dallas to *Where*?" 13

2 "Through the Looking Glass" 31

3 "His Wife Was a Firecracker" 41

4 "God Uses Unlikely People" 51

5 "A Gift from God and a Few New Friends" 59

6 "Christmas and The Newlyweds" 69

7 "The Lady in Lavender" 77

8 "The Sins of the Fathers, and a Little Cedar Tree" 89

9 "He Hates Pastors" 97

10 "Just Up the Road" 109

11 "Silver and Black '57" 123

12	"Day Is Done"	131
13	"Displaced Southerners"	141
14	"It's a 'Buht'!"	151
15	"L.C., That's Me!"	157
16	"You Always Say That!"	169
17	"Lord, Did We Step Out of Your Will?"	181
18	"Yes, Dear!"	187
19	"Snakes in the Basement"	199
20	"We've Got So Many Ways You're Bound to Like Some of Them."	207
21	"Three Weddings and a Funeral"	219
22	"Life in the Real World"	239

A Word from the Author

Writer, literary editor, and British punctuation–Nazi Lynne Truss wrote:

> My book was aimed at the tiny minority of British people 'who love punctuation and don't like to see it mucked about with'. When my own mother suggested we print on the front of the book 'For the select few,' I was hurt, I admit it; I bit my lip and blinked a tear. Yet I knew what she meant. I'm the writer, after all, who once wrote a whole comic novel about Lewis Carroll and Alfred, Lord Tennyson and expected other people to be interested. Oh yes, I have learned that lesson the hard way.[1]

I have few illusions, as Master Johannes De Silentio well states:

> The present writer is nothing of a philosopher; he is . . . an amateur writer. . . . He writes because for him it is a luxury which becomes the more agreeable and more evident, the fewer there are who buy and read what he writes. He can easily foresee his fate in an

---

[1] Lynne Truss, *Eats, Shoots & Leaves*, (New York: Gotham Books, 2003), xviii–xix.

age when passion has been obliterated in favor of learning, [or when learning has been obliterated in favor of passion] in an age when an author who wants to have readers must take care to write in such a way that the book can easily be perused during the afternoon nap [Though I do write what can be perused in an afternoon!], and take care to fashion his outward deportment in likeness to the picture of that polite young gardener in the advertisement sheet, who with hat in hand, and with a good certificate from the place where he last served, recommends himself to the esteemed public. He foresees his fate—that he will be entirely ignored.[2]

I identify with the words of Sartre about the writing process:

Genius is only a loan; it must be merited by great suffering, tested by ordeals that must be accepted modestly and firmly. One ends by hearing voices and writes at their dictation.[3]

---

[2] Søren Kierkegaard, *Fear and Trembling* and *The Sickness unto Death*, trans. Walter Lowrie (Princeton: Princeton University Press, 1941), 24. Johannes De Silentio was a pseudonym of Kierkegaard.
[3] Jean-Paul Sartre, *The Words* (Greenwich, CT: Fawcett Publications, Inc., 1964), 39.

Preface

Visiting the Yorkshire Dales in England was one of the items on my bucket list. While a driving tour of the Dales came a few years later, the initial foray was in 2006 when I went in the company of one of my college roommates, David Puckett. We rode the train north from London and took a taxi into Thirsk from the rail station outside of town. We wandered, and I gawked. The main place of interest was the museum in the former veterinary clinic of Alf Wight, alias James Herriot, of *All Creatures Great and Small* fame. Puckett took my picture with my arm up the nether end of a fake cow. There is another photo of me standing beside the mannequin-like figure of Mrs. Pumphrey, the favorite client of the trio of veterinarians of *All Creatures* fame. In one photo I am sitting in the old jalopy that James drove up hill and down dale through the scenic countryside around Thirsk.

On a subsequent trip we drove from north to south through the Dales one afternoon. Most of what we saw was disturbingly lonely and bereft of trees. The scattered barns and houses on the barren hills seemed separated by desolate miles.

My wife and I had delighted in the BBC series over the last thirty-five years, and my mind was filled with expectations of green pastures corralled by stone walls. We somehow missed the babbling brooks splashing gaily over the dips in the roads, the long and low stone walls, the ancient church ruins silhouetted against the sky.

Oh, don't get me wrong. There were lots of stone walls. Field stones were gathered together and wisely used to subdivide the fields and pastures. Afterall, the stones had to be put somewhere. But my mind was blending scenes from Wordsworth's "Tintern Abbey" with the opening moments of the BBC classic. Wordsworth had me looking for . . .

> These plots of cottage-ground, these orchard-tufts,
> Which at this season, with their unripe fruits,
> Are clad in one green hue, and lose themselves
> 'Mid groves and copses. Once again I see
> These hedge-rows, hardly hedge-rows, little lines
> Of sportive wood run wild: these pastoral farms,
> Green to the very door; and wreaths of smoke
> Sent up, in silence, from among the trees!
> With some uncertain notice, as might seem
> Of vagrant dwellers in the houseless woods,
> Or of some Hermit's cave, where by his fire
> The Hermit sits alone.[4]

---

[4] William Wordsworth, "Lines Composed a Few Miles above Tintern Abbey, On Revisiting the Banks of the Wye during a Tour. July 13, 1798," Poetry Foundation, Accessed June 21, 2022, https://www .poetryfoundation.org/poems/45527/lines-composed-a-few-miles-

Already I digress, and you are just getting to know me! Gentle reader, what *will* you think?

In my former forty years, successively pastoring three churches in the Plains and the Midwest, I visited with hundreds of parishioners over coffee and coffins. Doubts and fears, discouragement and wild joys, through births and dearth, in homes and on highways and in hospitals, I sought to encourage, to support, and to shepherd. I smiled and I wept and I supported and I encouraged and I confronted and I counseled and I exhorted and I laughed out loud. I have had great joys, and I have been sorely depressed. I have loved the ministry, and I have hated the ministry. Most of what I relate here reflects the former, but I know of no pastor who would be honest in saying there was never a time when he or she struggled, or never a time when she or he almost bowed to despair.

But let's not dwell on that. After all, in this era of walking in the shadow of the Pandemic and the Powder Keg, of inflation and recession or deflation and worse, one of my goals in writing this book is to offer to the reader a respite from the day-to-day dread[5] and the heightened unease so many have experienced. One of my chief aims is that my readers have the opportunity to sit and placidly

---

above-tintern-abbey-on-revisiting-the-banks-of-the-wye-during-a-tour-july-13-1798.

[5] When Jesus was soon to die, He sought to comfort and instill courage in His disciples with the promise of the coming Comforter and with these words: "Peace I leave with you, my peace I give unto you: not as the world gives, give I unto you. Let not your heart be troubled, neither let it be afraid" (John 14:27, Authorized Version).

read. But that is not enough. I want them to read, and as they read, I want them to find themselves . . . smiling. That's it! No lofty goals. I'm satisfied with your smiles.

A great many people have shared with me a great many things over the years. Anything that I have shared in this book is, in a figurative sense, past the "statute of limitations." What I mean by that is that many of the persons of whom I speak in this book are no longer living. In a few cases, I have changed the names of the individuals mentioned. In some cases I sought the permission of the individuals for their inclusion. In a few other cases, perhaps I should have sought the permission of individuals for their inclusion, and it did not occur to me to do so. I hope that they will pardon me. Sincerely!

This book purports to be a book about parishioners, but it clearly has to be about my own personal interactions with parishioners, so the book also is, to some extent, about me and my relationships and experiences in the churches I have pastored. My next book will be *All Preachers Great and Small.* Maybe. I mainly just wanted to establish that title as my own. Remember, you read it here first!

A final note: there are times when I mention details about finances and financial stress. Someone might think I have lived with a singular focus on money rather than ministry. For some, that would confirm what they think of preachers: that they are in it for the money. A little research could confirm that many pastors struggle to make ends meet. Many pastors and their wives, in former days, chose not to be a two-income family. My experience very likely reflects that of many pastors in America, especially in rural America. And after all, I am in rural America!

I am now in my retirement in central Missouri, but I still have a love for the Church and for the pastors who give their lives to the ministry. Most pastors do not have celebrity status, nor do they have celebrity salaries. The bulk of the churches in America have fewer than 100 in attendance on the average Sunday. *Christianity Today* relayed this information:

> A new study from Exponential by LifeWay Research found 6 in 10 Protestant churches are plateaued or declining in attendance . . . . The research gives a clear picture of the state of Protestant churches in America today. Most have fewer than 100 people attending services each Sunday (57%), including 21 percent who average fewer than 50. Around 1 in 10 churches (11%) average 250 or more for their worship services. Three in five (61%) pastors say their churches faced a decline in worship attendance or growth of 5 percent or less in the last three years. Almost half (46%) say their giving decreased or stayed the same from 2017 to 2018.[6]

Virtually all of the pastors I have known have been faithful to their spouses and are faithful servants of the Church and of the Lord Jesus Christ. The general public is much more aware of the "breaking bad" pastors who make the headlines for outrageous and immoral

---

[6] Aaron Earls, "Small, Struggling Congregations Fill U.S. Church Landscape," Lifeway Research, Lifeway Christian Resources, Accessed May 29, 2022, https://research.lifeway.com/2019/03/06/small-struggling-congregations-fill-u-s-church-landscape/.

behavior.[7] The bulk of the pastors in America are humble and loving servants who care little for notoriety or wealth. Those are the pastors whom I love, and they and their people are the ones I particularly wish to serve in this book.

I have no illusions about the reaction a book like this might engender. Almost none! "The world will little note, nor long remember what we say here, . . ."[8]

Some will read these words and imagine that I am arguing for a return to a former time and place. Jay Heinrichs mentions concerning *nostalgia* that a Swiss doctor coined the term to describe the ailment (*algia*) suffered by seventeenth-century Swiss mercenaries—homesickness. He explains: "The word comes from the Greek *nostos* (to return home) and *algia* (pain)."[9] Heinrichs continues: "The problem is, nostalgia not only distorts reality, turning the college years into halcyon days and the sixties South into Mayberry; the emotion also focuses on the wrong tense."[10] In mentioning "tense,"

---

[7] Stephanie Pagones, "Indiana woman...," Fox News, Accessed May 31, 2022, https://www.foxnews.com/us/indiana-pastor-sex-congregant-bobi-gephart-john-lowe-new-life-church-warsaw.

[8] A. Lincoln was quite wrong when he summed up that address in Gettysburg, Nov. 19, 1863. I am a white male. I write from that standpoint and from the worldview of conservative Christianity. My doing so does not mean that I denigrate every other viewpoint and worldview. My goal is to be kind and to encourage those who happen to read my writings.

[9] Jay Heinrichs, *Thank You for Arguing: What Aristotle, Lincoln, and Homer Simpson Can Teach Us about the Art of Persuasion,* (New York: Three Rivers Press, 2017), 96.

[10] Ibid.

Heinrichs suggests the need to focus on the future rather than the past.

Who am I kidding?[11] Certainly not anyone who might chance to read this book. Most of them, like me, will think of the former days as days of glory—with a measure of wholesomeness and wholeness thrown in. Most of them think they grew up in Mayberry! And they rode their bicycles safely all over Mayberry! To all hours!

Oh, and I also should mention this. One of my heroes is Onesiphorus. Remember him? He was a bit player in the New Testament. He was one of those courageous and humble and unselfish and caring individuals who encouraged the heart of the great Apostle Paul.

Paul was the New Testament tough guy. He probably grew up in Brooklyn or Queens. He did not suffer fools gladly,[12] as they say. He was generally short on patience and had quite an aggressive personality. Enter Onesiphorus. He was not the winner of the Boston Marathon. He was the one who stood on Heartbreak Hill and urgently extended a paper cup of water to the frontrunner.

I want to be as useful to the Lord as Onesiphorus was. Paul says of him in 2 Timothy 1:19 that "he often refreshed me and was not ashamed of my chains, . . ." The Greek word for "refresh" is picturesque. It speaks of

---

[11] Will someone prefer that I write "Whom am I kidding?" I sometimes write colloquially, and at other times, more formally.
[12] 2 Corinthians 11:19 says that the Corinthians *did* "suffer fools gladly" (AV).

"breathing again." It suggests to me an image of someone holding another up and supporting him so that he can catch a breath.

Onesiphorus was one of those persons of whom we say: "He was a breath of fresh air." Lord, help me be that to those who read.

This book is dedicated to my wife, the adorable and lovely Wesley Heard Brown. It is quite possible that she will be the subject of a future book, if the Lord tarries. David Puckett called one day and offered the title of this book. The proffered title provided the needed spur to launch this project. I wrote furiously for two months, and this book is the result.

If I ever write the book All Preachers Great and Small, two of the great ones will be my two pastors. Both have been my friends and my mentors for most of my life: Jerry Clark and Ken Sheppard.

Melissa Backe Howard was the Good Grammaritan[13] and sought to guide me and warn me from danger as I typed. If you object to what I have written, she and anyone else mentioned in these pages must be absolved of any guilt. All errors of every type are, alas, my own!

Ah! One more thing! My wife calls me "Brown Eddie." A mutual friend introduced me to her with that

---

[13] If others may be grammarphobes and punctuation-Nazis, Melissa is the ultimate Good Grammaritan. And, yes, I love to make up my own words when I need one.

appellation. The story behind that will likely be in the next book.

Wes and I live just outside of Sedalia, Missouri. Our hobby farm we call Brown Acres, and there we are privileged to live with six collies, twelve chickens, one cat, and nineteen too many goats.

Here is a picture of the author preparing for his trip to England in 2006. A separate suitcase contained bottled water.

Chapter One

"From Dallas to *Where*?"

One Friday night in May of 1979, half a dozen of my family and a few close friends came to a large auditorium in Dallas to watch me walk across a stage in a rented black robe. I was graduating after four years in a master's program at Dallas Theological Seminary. The following day we all went out to eat as the celebration and visit continued. When Monday morning came, I went back to my job as a lowly courier in downtown Dallas.

While many of my classmates went off to pursue Ph.D.'s and many others went on to pastorates across the States and Canada, I was called to 4700 First International Building. That was the office of Hewitt, Johnson, Swanson and Barbee, and I was to "RUSH" a package to someone named Ray Hunt. He was about to board a plane at DFW for some high-powered business merger or acquisition or mega-deal. Did you catch his last name?

Before the age of cell phones, I was rushing up Stemmons Freeway toward the connecting highway to the airport. My beeper buzzed furiously three times in a row. When all three fifteen-second messages were connected, they warned me not to have Mr. Hunt paged . . . "because of who he is." They further described him as having blondish hair and a tan-colored suit. I screeched my little Wingtip Courier Honda Civic to an abrupt halt and parked it in the standing zone in front of the terminal. I hopped out and ran inside, placing the package like a baton in the outstretched hand of the runner of the next leg, Mr. Ray Hunt himself. And off he flew, and so did I.

And that's the sort of thing that I did with my master's degree in the study of the Old Testament and the Hebrew language.

Ken, a friend of mine, owned the business and operated it out of his apartment for a few months. As his client list grew, he took the bold step of renting an office in downtown Dallas. It was in the third or fourth tallest building at that time, and our office was some fifteen stories up. One of his good friends, a retired African American woman named Ethel, volunteered to serve as office manager. Whenever a call would come from a client, she would relay the message to one of the three couriers via a beeper that could announce that fifteen second message. The message would contain the client's name, the address of the pickup, and the nature of the delivery. Clients paid extra for RUSH deliveries.

On one special occasion, I had made a delivery and had not been given another assignment. I had parked the car in the parking garage under our building and was stuffed into the elevator with half a dozen secretaries and their bosses as they returned from lunch. The elevator was jostling and speeding up the shaft when my beeper went off with Ethel's mellifluously commanding voice: "Eddie! Where in the hell are you?" No one was convinced when I looked around the elevator as though trying to find the source of the eruption.

It was probably about 1:30 in the afternoon, and every day about that time, the courier business would take a siesta. It was an absolutely dead time. Everyone in the business world had gone to lunch, and no contracts or architectural drawings had been generated. Ken knew his bills continued whether the deliveries did or not, and every day at that same time he would go into his inner office to bemoan his fate. Like the suffering biblical character Job, he would curse the day he was born.[14] Ethel, Dave, and I could hear the loud crying and shrieks coming from inside his office. Eventually, Ethel would speak soothingly to him, and she would regularly utter these words: "All sickness is not death." Somewhere around 2:30, every day, the courier business would spring alive again.

I had worked for Ken during my last semester of seminary, and upon graduation, I became his first full-time employee. He was due a vacation, and before he took

---

[14] Job 3. Jeremiah did the same: Jer. 20:14 (AV).

a week's vacation, he dubbed me Assistant Manager of Wingtip Couriers. That title gave me the authority, upon his order, to fire one of our employees, another lowly seminary graduate, who wasn't working out well. He had been losing his temper with clients, and that was costing us business. The termination was a sign from God that he was to pursue his Ph.D., which he did, and I continued to deliver packages.

But I was not just a seminary graduate without a real job; I was also a college graduate without a real job. I had studied English Literature, Philosophy, Psychology, Sociology, Anthropology, Theology, Counseling, Greek, and Hebrew. And I was working for a few dollars an hour in a dead-end job.

In addition to that, I was pretty low on the list of potential pastors graduating from Dallas Seminary. That was so, in part, because I had not majored in the conventional course of study that churned out pastors there. A major in Old Testament was often a prelude to a Ph.D. program in the United Kingdom or a respected stateside university. I could be wrong, but it seemed that the ones who went sailing with ease through Bob Salstrom's Office of Placement at the seminary were majors in Pastoral Ministries or English Bible. But what did I know? I couldn't check that theory with others of my classmates. Everyone else had already moved on with life and career while I delivered packages for $3.50 an hour and at about ten miles per hour over the speed limit.

Then one day in October I heard from Bob Salstrom's secretary. I was to go to a little town in northern Oklahoma to "candidate." That meant that I was to go and try out for the position of pastor. The date was assigned, and I began to plan our trip. It was 300 miles north of Dallas, so for a southern boy from Mississippi, it was "up north." The only intelligence I had about the small church was that Gerry, one of my classmates, had recently visited the church to candidate. As a Pastoral Ministries major, he was well-prepared and knew what to look for in a church in terms of its prospects for growth and success. The church had voted him in with a large percentage of the vote, but he had turned them down.

If Tonkawa Bible Church had been a Baptist church, it could have been dubbed "Bleak Prospects Baptist Church." And the bleak prospects were what Gerry had seen and had turned down. What that church needed was an Old Testament major who didn't know any better.

On a cold and gray Saturday afternoon in December, Wes and I drove the six hours from Dallas to Tonkawa for me to preach and interview over the weekend. My wife's name is Wesley, and most people call her "Wes," except for her family and her Mississippi Delta cousins who call her "Wessie Jean."

The further north we went, the cloudier and darker it became.

Just before crossing the bridge on the south side of Tonkawa, Wes and I saw in our headlights a weed tumbling across the highway. We looked at each other and said, "Tumbleweed." We had never seen one of those before. Suddenly I felt like I was entering Dodge City or the set for *Gunsmoke.*

We had spoken by telephone to Joe Marshall, one of the elders of Tonkawa Bible Church, and he had given us directions to the Western Auto store on Grand Avenue in Tonkawa. There we met the kindly old gentleman with the well-worn, pleated slacks drawn tight with a leather belt and held high, . . . well, high like older men often wear their 20-year-old slacks.

The Western Auto store was a hardware store that carried a variety of items for the car and the home. Joe's store had antique toys in original packaging. He and Mabel eked out a meager existence and most months made enough, I believe, to pay the bills. On the wall above the cash register was a gun collection with a few going back to Civil War days and beyond. In the back of the store was a large hand-and-pulley-operated lift that went to the top floor and the basement. In two conspicuous places, there were fake cameras with a glowing red light, just to make a potential shoplifter stop and think.

Joe asked if we had eaten. He then closed up shop and walked us a few doors down to Mary's Cafe. It was 5:30 in the wintertime, and the lights were shining on Grand Avenue.

Joe Marshall was a soft-spoken, humble man with glasses, white hair, and a pleasant smile. I suppose I was ready to move to Tonkawa about 5 minutes after I met Joe, but when we visited over supper, I was completely sold. Already I could see myself in that small Oklahoma town. It was only slightly larger than my hometown in Mississippi. Joe then asked if we had seen the church. No, we had gone directly to meet him when we arrived.

It was the middle of December, cold and breezy, like every winter night in northern Oklahoma. We followed Joe down the brick street with rough and raised patches of asphalt, and the roar of the tires got louder as we got up to speed on the brickwork. Joe drove a handful of blocks and stopped under an elm tree beside a lovely stone structure with a tower and a greenish-gray slate roof. The stained-glass windows in that church were valuable works of art. Over the door was a concrete relief depicting an open Bible bearing the words from John's Gospel, "Thy Word Is Truth." It was, without contest, the most beautiful building in town.

Tonkawa Bible Church

Once inside, Joe flicked the light switch and then held tightly to the railing and lowered himself down the steep stairs. We followed in the dim and yellow light. On came other lights as we walked through the musty basement, and Joe turned on the big boiler that was in the room just through and beyond the men's room. The boiler heated an antifreeze-type fluid that ran through copper piping in the concrete floor of the sanctuary. The next morning the temperature was perfect.

Just off the furnace room Joe found and grabbed a big push broom of the dry mop type. He then went forth and back on the floors in the basement. I got the broom and dustpan and swept up his findings. And then, slowly, he made his way back up the steep stairs in the rear of the church building to sweep the sanctuary.

He went between the pews and swiveled the dust mop around each pew end to conserve the results. In one spot at the back of the church he would shake the dust off the mop and begin again where he had left off. Every few minutes this 78-year-old heart patient would stop, place both hands at the top of the mop, and lean on the sturdy mop handle to breathe for a moment. Then he would begin again.

Joe Marshall was an elder in this small church with barely 40 people on a "good" Sunday morning. He, along with Mr. Ernest Wetmore, had founded the church the year I was born. There was little money to pay a pastor, and no money to pay a janitor, and there was no one else who seemed to volunteer to serve in cleaning the church. So one of the best men I have ever known was the one who weekly would clean the church when he got off work on Saturday night.

From the lovely church building we went to an older part of the old town to the home of Joe and Mabel. Sitting on a small lot with overgrown bushes crowding the walls and the eaves, it had gray-asbestos shingles and a small front porch. In the spring it was surrounded by beautiful pink and white and red peonies, but in the winter, it was drab and gray like the sky.

Ushered into our room where we would spend the night, we set our suitcase down in the cramped space lately used for storage and overflow. After meeting Mabel, we were introduced to several cats of the Manx variety—cats with no tails. Joe and Mabel would amuse themselves and the cats with a piece of wide and flexible ribbon attached to a dowel rod with a string. They would flick the ribbon on the rod, and the cats would never tire of attacking and clawing the ribbon. I had never been in a home with cats before. I discovered that wherever one sat one might be sitting on a cushion of cat hair.

The next morning came early with coffee proffered with juice and a substance of which I had never heard. It was something called "Malt-O-Meal," and to make up for its lack of salt and butter and taste, there was an overflowing abundance of it in the gargantuan bowl placed before me. Had I not been a bit nervous, it still would have been much too much for my five-foot, nine-and-one-half-inch, 156-pound frame.

Mabel was more white-headed than her husband, but some childhood ailment had left her with a slight limp, and it was hard to imagine that she ever felt very well. A slightly aquiline nose presided over her . . . I hate to say it . . . sourly downturned lips.

The church knew they were running out of options, so any young seminary graduate looked good to them. Even one who was balding prematurely! Their desperate situation made me a virtual shoo-in. Counting me as a likely-to-be-hired young pastor, Mabel began that morning at breakfast to educate us about the two grocery stores in Tonkawa, Dorsett's and Food World. Mabel refused to shop at Dorsett's because they sold beer, but she would go there for bananas because their bananas were better than those at Food World. Mabel was just as inconsistent in her thinking as the rest of us. Well, maybe she was a bit more so!

Moments later I was putting on my suit to go to Tonkawa Bible Church to meet the small flock which I would shepherd for the next five and a half years. I brushed off the cat hair from my suit-bag. I unzipped it. I was terror-struck!

As a pastor for four decades, one of my recurring nightmares over those years was that 10:30 Sunday morning had come, and I was not ready to preach. I lived out that nightmare virtually EVERY WEEK for some 38 years. Understand, in the early days I would put in the recommended 20 hours of preparation for a Sunday morning sermon.[15] That involved a careful translation of the passage from the original language, a study of the text and scrupulous notetaking on the passage, and finally

---

[15] Haddon Robinson "wrote the book" on preaching. Most conservative seminaries used his textbook, *Biblical Preaching*, in their homiletics classes. Dallas Seminary students were privileged to have him as their professor, and the process of preparation for preaching that he prescribed involved a twenty-hour commitment.

the arrival at the interpretive outline which preceded the homiletical (preaching) outline of the passage. At that point I would turn to the commentaries and works of theology for comments on the passage I was to preach. Finally, I would begin to manuscript the message, beginning with an introduction in which I was seeking to orient the hearer to the subject I believed the biblical passage was teaching. Each major point would be illustrated with a story, some current topic in the news, or a fact or object that would bring light to the subject, since that is what "illustrate" means.

Religiously, I would conclude my manuscript by 12:30 PM on the Friday before it was to be preached. On Saturday morning, in the early days, I would go to the church and stand in the pulpit and fairly read the sermon into a tape recorder. I would preach the sermon with gestures I anticipated using when the entire congregation of some 35 to 40 parishioners arrived on Sunday morning to be enlightened and enlivened and prepared for the week ahead of them. And on Sunday morning at 5:30 I would listen to the sermon on tape while I bathed and shaved, and then I would pore over it for another three hours until I left for church to teach Sunday School an hour before I was to preach.

And yet, I still did not feel ready.

The problem was that I am the sort of person that never FEELS ready. I may be ready, but I am always the last one to know. In the very real night-time nightmare that I have from time to time, I am preaching in a place that is unfamiliar to me. I lack my sermon outline, or worse, some article of clothing. Sometimes it's just a tie that I lack, but sometimes it's a shirt or shoes—or, gulp . . . pants.

And on that Sunday morning as I was putting on my suit, it was an hour before Sunday School started that I realized I had not packed a tie when we came from Dallas.

I panicked! Dear, elderly Joe Marshall brought in a large selection of ties from which I could choose. This collection had been gathered over the course of some sixty years, and there were several patterns and widths. They were stylish in former decades, and they had been in existence long enough to have come in and gone out of style more than once. There were paisleys, stripes, solids, and GRAVY STAINS. Thankfully none of them remotely matched my suit, so Joe Marshall called one of the young men of the congregation (45-year-old Don Hiebert) who brought his selection of ties to church. I found one that matched admirably. BUT IT IS AN AWFUL FEELING NOT TO FEEL READY FOR AN IMPORTANT APPOINTMENT!

After the sermon, there was a great deal of smiling and glad-handing and covered dishes and desserts and questions for me and for Wes. Wes was her typical winsome self, and she has often been called my best asset as a pastor.

That night the church voted to call me as its pastor. I would be the seventh pastor in a ten-year period. Pastors didn't last long at Tonkawa Bible Church in those days. In fact, the pastor who preceded me had whispered too loudly to someone that the "church could go places" if they "could have a few, good funerals." For some reason, several of those slated for funerals were not quite ready for their life's summary to be shared in the obituaries, and the pastor was encouraged to move along down the road. Prior to that pastor was one who had lasted a respectable three years before he and his family were called to a larger church in a larger town by the name of Dallas.

Wes and I were quite in love with the little church with its country and small-town folk. A month later, my parents helped us load a U-Haul trailer, and Dad pulled it north from Dallas to Tonkawa. That was a Monday. When Wednesday morning came, Mother and Dad were on their way back to Brandon, Mississippi. That's the town which I have claimed for years had at the city limits the sign which read: "Boyhood Home of Eddie Brown." (Perhaps it is not there now after all these years. Also, there is every possibility in the South that the sign is no longer visible having been overcome by Kudzu many years ago.)

That first Wednesday night in Tonkawa I remember feeling abandoned. There was some high, lonesome feeling like I was finally an adult and that I had assumed the responsibility for the course of Wes's and my future.

I suppose I had felt something similar four and a half years earlier when Mother and Dad had helped us move to Dallas in August of 1975. Wes and I had been married for a couple of months, and then we found ourselves in a new city in an apartment complex with a couple of dozen other seminary couples.

The first week of seminary had been brutal. Assignments for the semester were in the syllabus for each class. I had worked compulsively to finish the first week's assignments by Thursday afternoon so that I could have an evening off. We had our dinner together, and Wes was off to her first "Wives Fellowship."

Each Thursday evening, seminary wives would gather in Chafer Chapel for lectures from popular seminary professors. There was singing, prayer, orientation to seminary life, the announcements of events pertinent to the wives of seminary students, and the occasional skit. Wes was soon selected to be a regular in the skits at Wives Fellowship. She was in her element, but on that first Thursday evening, I was exhausted, especially mentally exhausted.

I left the seminary and drove aimlessly down historic Swiss Avenue toward White Rock Lake. After one week of classes, I was burned out. I had stayed up late and had risen early. I had worked at a frenetic pace, and, as Milton put it, I had "scorned delights and lived laborious days."[16] It was not until after some 30 years of marriage that Wes called me an "old stick in the mud," but that first week, I was well on my way to becoming just that.

I parked the car by the lakeshore and walked over to the lake. Ducks were panhandling with every passerby, and I stood and stared at the lake as the sun sank low. I began aimlessly to throw rocks to skim them across the surface. I grimly wondered if I had made a mistake. Was

---

[16] John Milton, "Lycidas," line 74, Poetry Foundation, Accessed October 1, 2022, https://www.poetryfoundation.org/poems/44733/lycidas.

I able to do the work required in graduate school? What made life more miserable was my inability to let on that I was doubting my intellect and my academic abilities. I believe I was in an environment in which many felt the same self-doubt, but no one wanted to be the first to admit that there was something about theology or the Bible which he or she did not understand. But wasn't that the very reason we were attending seminary—to learn about theology and the Bible?

Many incoming seminarians attend seminary because it is a necessary step on the career path, and, truth be known, many of them are quite content that there is very little they do not know. At least that is the case until they complete their first week of seminary, and then they begin to suspect that there is very little that they do know! From knowing everything to knowing nothing in less than a week: quite the period of enlightenment! They have never learned such an important lesson in so short a period of time.

Four more years and a master's Thesis! Could I do it? Well, dear reader, you read the opening lines of this book, and you know the outcome. I even graduated with honors! But still, I wonder. If I could feel this uncertain about myself and my abilities, is it possible that others in various fields feel similarly? Do other people deal with some of the same struggles I had and have? I believe that they do. Do other people in this big world have some of the same ideals and desires in life that I do? I believe that they do. I am writing this book for them.

Back in Tonkawa on that first Wednesday night at Tonkawa Bible Church, I led those who attended our prayer meeting in a reflection of Psalm 27:7-10.

> Hear, O LORD, when I cry with my voice, And be gracious to me and answer me. *When You said,* "Seek My face," my heart said to You, "Your face, O LORD, I shall seek." Do not hide Your face from me, Do not turn Your servant away in anger; You have been my help; Do not abandon me nor forsake me, O God of my salvation! For my father and my mother have forsaken me, But the LORD will take me up.[17]

I had been drawn to that passage because it reflected the feeling of abandonment I had felt. I had felt it when I first arrived in the new situation in seminary, and I felt it again as I faced the reality of adulthood in another new life situation. I could only call out to the Lord. Even now, as I write at the age of seventy, still, I can only call out to the Lord in my uncertainties and insecurities. He is faithful!

On our second Friday night in Tonkawa, Joe and Mabel Marshall invited us and Gladys Shelhamer to accompany them to the open house of the new fire station. It was a glorious event in the life of our little town of Tonkawa. We met a few people and drank punch with our cookies, and we were safe and sound at home by 6:30. Wes and I sat in the front room of the parsonage[18] and looked at each other. Maybe there was not much to do in

---

[17] New American Standard Bible
[18] A parsonage is a residence supplied by the church for a pastor of the church.

a small town, and we didn't know anyone yet—at least we did not know anyone our ages. After all, considering ourselves in the computation, the average age of the parishioners was sixty-five!

The next day we went eight miles up the road to Walmart and bought our first television for $120, a 19" black-and-white wonder. We watched *Dukes of Hazzard* on Friday nights, and on Sunday nights after church, we were introduced to our favorite series of all time . . . the British-produced *All Creatures Great and Small.* We strained to follow the dialogue of the young Scottish veterinarian in the Yorkshire Dales of England, but we were delighted by the indecipherable accents and the antics of the clientele of James Herriot and one of the greatest characters in television history: Siegfried Farnon, M.R.C.V.S.[19]

---

[19] Member of the Royal College of Veterinary Surgeons. The original production featured Robert Hardy as Siegfried Farnon. *All Creatures Great and Small,* written by Johnny Byrne and Ted Rhodes, created and produced by Bill Sellars, 1978–1990, BBC1.

Chapter Two

"Through the Looking Glass"

One evening I had gotten home to the parsonage across the back alley from the church. I was seated on the couch in the front room when I heard a positive roar. Our front door was of wood and encased a five-foot-by-two-foot sheet of thick glass, beveled at the edges. It was easy to see out, and that, of course, made it easy to see in! I guessed that the roaring sound was from the corner of 1st and Grand, coming around the corner by the church.

I ran to the front door to see the muscle car that was careering up the street. It was a shiny black Camaro with yellow and orange flames painted on the side by the front wheel wells. It swerved into place and stopped abruptly across the street and north. A tall young man got out and ran up the few steps to the house on the corner. Hmmm! Who could that be?

Larry's hot Camaro

I was home for lunch another day. Across the street and to the left a bit was a man washing a flat white, utilitarian pickup with a whitish camper top. Now is as good a time as any.

"Hi, I'm your new neighbor. I'm Eddie Brown."

"Bob Martin. Nice to meet you."

Bob was a rural mail carrier and was a man of routine. He arose early each morning and was off to the post office, arriving, if my memory serves, at 6:30 AM each day. By 1:35 PM he was home, and by 1:40 he was washing his truck. Every day the water would wash off the rust-brown dust from the roads of Kay County. The water would run down the street to a muddy reservoir in front of the house of Mr. Joe and Mr. Jim Creasey. The Creaseys were almost directly across from us. Bob had a well in his backyard, so he had all the water he wanted, and he had a clean pickup for a few hours every day.

Very soon Wes was able to meet the lady of the hot-rod house on the corner. Reta was Bob and Billie's daughter, and she was married to the owner of the Green

Light Auto Store. Ahhhh! That made sense. Larry Swords, a parts store guy, drove the hot Camaro. Every visitor to the Green Light Auto Store was made to feel welcome upon entry. Larry would shout, "Hi, Handsome! What can I do for you?"

Out the front door I could see Mr. Jim Creasey come and go in his pickup, but Mr. Joe Creasey came out the front door to feed his collection of cats, and then he went back inside. This was repeated a couple of times a day. He didn't say much.

Our neighbors to the north were the Frielings, and Weldon was the local policeman. Between us was the church playground that consisted of a few well-built swings and a couple of seesaws from the 1950s. Dividing the properties was a row of walnut trees that poisoned Wes's garden each year.

In early April the drab town came to life with jonquils and buttercups. The trees were in bloom and budding, and the grass and the green onions were shooting up. The parsonage came equipped with a push mower: a 22-inch, 3.5 hp Briggs and Stratton. It was pushed up underneath the add-on back porch of the parsonage to keep the engine out of the weather. All I needed was gas, because everyone knows you never have to change the oil in a Briggs and Stratton engine. They start the first pull, every time. Pretty soon I noticed that the strip of grass and onions in front of the church had not been mowed. Well, I could get that done in fifteen minutes, and about forty-five minutes for the yard of the parsonage was sufficient.

As a first-time pastor, I was learning what the contract meant by "other duties."

In May the peonies were in full bloom, and the little town was a sight to behold and to enjoy. All the way down Grand to the east was Northern Oklahoma College. Each evening Wes and I would go for walks. The sidewalks were inconsistent, occasional broken pieces of concrete surrounded by dirt and daring weeds. We would amble back and forth between the streets and the sidewalks. There were three college professors in our little church, and one of them, at 38, was the youngest man in the church, not counting 27-year-old me, of course. Tom and his family lived a few blocks south of us. They had three beautiful children and were an engaging couple.

They lived on a shaded corner just past an attractive and well-kept house with a gambrel-style roof. It was neatly painted, and it always caught my eye. I liked to walk down that block just to see it.

Across town was the Hiebert family, Don and Virginia with their three daughters and one son. It was a delight to be invited to their home for dinner. Virginia was a nurse who loved to read. She shared her complete collection of Agatha Christie novels with us. When I added *The Complete Works of Sherlock Holmes* and *The Lord of the Rings,* I had bedtime reading for a couple of years. Don was a business professor at the local college. They had not always lived in town. They had moved in a few years before our arrival.

Tonkawa is situated some twenty miles from Kansas in the far north, center of the state, and it is in the parallelogram that runs from north Texas into southeastern Kansas where there are more tornadoes per square mile than anywhere else on the planet. In Kay County, the average annual rainfall is 32 inches per year, and going west or east from there in Oklahoma, the approximate, average rainfall can be computed by adding two inches of rain for every 15 miles eastward and subtracting two inches every 15 miles westward.

No other place I ever lived had weather systems that were so fascinating. So many times the clouds would be roiling and boiling overhead, or a fast-moving system could be seen ten miles away sweeping across the plains and charging like a raging bull.

I remember once being south of Tonkawa in the early evening—some ten miles south and on a slight rise. A small but testy, perfectly contained system blew in over Tonkawa. The thunderstorm had flashes and rumblings, and all of its fury was circumscribed in a system barely four miles across. Another memorable system had wind gusts of 93 miles per hour. One Sunday morning during church, high winds rattled the roof vents, and three inches of rain fell in forty-five minutes while a small tornado skipped and hopped across the northwest part of our city limits. Then one night before the children went to bed, I was "rather indisposed" when I heard the tornado sirens wailing followed by the roar of a "freight train." I shouted to Wes: "Get my kids to the church basement!"

Only the week before, the National Weather Service had issued a tornado watch. Nothing had come of it. Our defenses were down, and Wes was reluctant to bother with herding up the children to take shelter.

As soon as I could, I opened the bathroom door and ran across the alley to the church to join my family in the basement! That tornado was mostly just sound and fury. It strutted and fretted in the treetops barely three blocks from our little home.

Some years before we knew the Hieberts, for once the five-day forecast had been right. Weathermen, you know, are honest men who can't be trusted.[20] The clouds began rolling in across the plains of northern Oklahoma. In spring through fall the weather around Tonkawa can be something to fear. It was October 1973, and Don and Virginia lived half a mile south of town on 75 acres. The Salt Fork River was their border on the east. They had been listening to the weather reports, and the one thing they didn't need was what was expected—more rain.

The four Hiebert children were snuggled away in bed—a two, a four, a six, and an eight-year-old. All were sleeping placidly, knowing nothing about the danger that awaited the Hiebert family.

Sometime that night the rain began. A hard rain. All day it had been raining upstream. The rain beat on the roof and kept Don and Virginia awake. The river, less than 200 yards from their house, was rising fast.

Perhaps Don got up to check—perhaps Don heard a noise—but the first sign of danger was the water gushing up through the toilet. Then it came under the front door— then under the back door. His feet were wet in the hall,

---

[20] The same is true for weatherwomen: they are honest women who can't be trusted!

and he knew it was time to leave. Maybe it was even past time to leave.

They rushed through the water to their car. Water was on the floorboard. Would the car start? THANK GOD IT DID! He maneuvered the car up the driveway to the road. He drove in high water toward town. He couldn't see the road—he couldn't see the ditch, but soon he found it—the ditch, that is.

All six scurried out of the car into the flowing, waist-high water. They were terrified. It was a nightmare. They made it back up to the road and waded back to their home. Once they were back to the house, they called the fire department in town. Rescuers drove through water across the bridge and took them back to the safety of the town.

All six of them were saved that night, and wherever they go for the rest of their lives, they will all remember that horrible night or the tales of it. Laurie, David, Susan, and Sherri will tell the story to their children and their grandchildren.

One day Pearl Wetmore, the benevolent matriarch of the church, called to say that Virginia was in the hospital in Ponca City. Ponca was about 20 minutes east of Tonkawa, and it was there that Conoco had a major presence as the largest employer in the area. This was my first hospital call as a pastor. Wes was free, and she wanted to go along to see Virginia. We found her in her hospital room with a slightly embarrassed smile. She was sitting up in bed with her shoulder in a horrid sling contraption. Virginia had fallen off a horse and had broken her shoulder. That was all I needed to know, thank you, but Wes has always had an unquenchable interest in things medical and dental. Even in gross things medical and dental! She had worked in Dallas as a dental assistant, but she would have made an interesting sort of nurse had she not become an unconventional pastor's wife.

Virginia was a registered nurse but also a professor in the nursing program at the local community college. She relished the opportunity to discuss her own condition in minute and thoroughly disgusting detail. She had seen the X-ray, and she began to describe it to Wes—and to me. I suppose I had gotten quiet. After all, this part of the visit was for Wes's and Virginia's enjoyment. I would offer a prayer for the patient at the end of our visit. Maybe. As Virginia offered excruciating details of the splintering of the bone and the scattered fragments and bits of bone and ripped and shredded cartilage visible in the X-ray or the CT scan, my eyes widened, but still I was speechless. The more minutely and picturesquely she described the nauseatingness of her condition, the less likely it became that I would offer even a short prayer. Wes was thoroughly engrossed in the conversation and had forgotten I was there. She drew her chair in closer to Virginia, their eyes flashing in mutual delight. And then Virginia, the nurse, saw that I needed help. I had turned a whiter shade of white. My jaw had dropped, and my mouth was as wide open as my eyes. For the second time in my life, I was about to faint. Virginia sprang into action. Well, from her restraints in the bed she commanded me to put my head down between my knees. I suppose it worked, and I can't imagine that I prayed with the patient before Wes helped me out of the hospital room and back to the car from my very first hospital visit as a young pastor.

One evening as we were preparing for our evening walk, I happened to be near the front door when I noticed a familiar pickup rolling past slowly. It was before the days when Google vehicles went up and down streets recording every outward detail of our personal property and space. I was a few feet from the door, but I could clearly see familiar faces looking out the driver's side window. All were looking through the glass front door directly into the parsonage. I was beginning to experience life in the fishbowl, as they say of the life of pastors.

Chapter Three

"His Wife Was a Firecracker"

After our candidating weekend among the people at Tonkawa, I went back one weekend to preach at the church on a Sunday in December. A good friend went along with me. While we were there, we went through the parsonage to discuss changes and fixups that might be made before our move in early January. Hugh Simmons was a big and stout farmer in the church. He was thinking about our move to Tonkawa, and he asked me if all of our belongings would fit into a "stawk trailer."

I am, of course, a Mississippian by birth. There are all sorts of slanders against my state, and I've heard many of them, but the one that stung the most was uttered by a fellow Dallas seminarian from Illinois. On the first day of one of my classes, we were going around the room introducing ourselves with our names and a few details such as where we were from, what college we attended, and our college major. I said, "I'm Eddie Brown, and I grew up in Mississippi. I went to Mississippi College and majored in English." Without a pause Phil said: "Oh, I didn't know they spoke English in Mississippi."

On the day Wes and I arrived in Dallas at our seminary apartment complex, we were unloading the trailer. Wes was first to meet the gentleman who was perched on the railing of the second floor. He watched us unload and carry items up the stairs to our apartment. He introduced himself to Wes. She asked Ken Quick where he was from.

"I'm from *WaRshington*, D.C."

And she said to Ken: "You tawk funny!"

Well, Hugh Simmons asked if all of our belongings would fit into a "stawk trailer" for our move to Tonkawa, Oklahoma. I had spent the first twelve years of my life going to my grandparents' farm virtually daily, but I had no idea what a "stawk trailer" was. I cocked my head sideways a bit, and I looked at Hugh over my right eyeglass lens. I carefully enunciated the words: "What's a . . . 'stawk trailer'? Do you mean like 'corn stalks'?"

Hugh was somewhat taken aback, and he seemed a bit miffed and flustered. He had failed in his attempt to communicate. He didn't try to explain. Hugh seemed to wonder where this young pastor was from, and what kind of sheltered life this *obvious* city boy had lived, but in addition to those questions, I think he wondered *just what kind of a pastor they were getting!*

Some time passed, and Hugh was talking to us about a farmer friend of his who had a son. The son went off to college and came home with an attitude along with his college degree.[21]

Once Hugh had told me about a farmer friend of his who was so strong he could walk up to a 55 gallon drum of oil, pick it up, and walk off with it. I believe they weigh some 450 pounds. I wonder if it was *that* farmer's son who had gone off to college.

One day the father of the college boy had put up with it as long as he could, but he grew tired of the supercilious attitude of the know-it-all son. He bellowed out: "Go over there and stick your hand in that 'stawk tank.' Now pull it out! How big a hole did it leave? That's how big a hole it would leave if you weren't around here." Well, it may have been a bit harsh, but it put the young man in his place. A "stawk tank" was a large, galvanized tank that held water for livestock, so I figured out that a "stawk trailer" was a "stock trailer." But that was some months later, so we moved to Tonkawa pulling a U-Haul trailer.

Whenever there was something wrong with the heating or the plumbing in the parsonage, Hugh was the designated fixer. He would pull up in his big ¾ ton pickup and park in the alley. His hands were huge and strong, and I'm sure he was able to twist off bolts with his bare hands. Each of his fingers were one and a half times the size of mine. His ample girth protruded beyond the bounds of his trousers and hid his belt buckle from his eyes and from the eyes of the world. He would smooth the thin strands of hair with his fingers and then hold them

---

[21] The alert reader might imagine that it was a Bachelor of Science degree!

in place with a hat supplied by a seed corn dealer. His smudged bifocals would slip down his nose, and he would have to push them back up his nose frequently. Hugh always seemed to bite his tongue a bit, and he wouldn't share with us the source of his amusement at our ways and abilities or the lack of them. But he was always amused at us, and it was obvious that he enjoyed interacting with Wes.

If Hugh happened to stop by my office to chat, he would sit across my office in a folding chair. He then invariably would pull out his pocketknife and begin to trim his fingernails. His knife was sharp enough to enable him to start on one side of each fingernail and cut off a rounded sliver. A sixteenth of an inch he would pare from each nail. I would be seated behind my desk dreading what was about to happen. After he had finished, he would have his knife blade still open at a right angle with the rest of the knife, and he would hold onto the knife by the bottom end of the knife. Holding the knife end between his thumb and forefinger, he would jab the sharp point of the blade at my eyes and would punctuate his sentences with a shake of the knife point toward my naked eyes.

I am not without my phobias, but one of my most significant ones, behind hatred of crawling in narrow passages in caves filled with bat poop and arachnids, is my phobia of sharp objects near my eyes. Or five feet away from my eyes but pointed toward my eyes! My naked eyes! Hugh would drive me to distraction, and I really and truly would cover my closed eyes with my hands as I turned away.

Hugh was a man of strong opinions. Of one dear lady who lived in fear that someone was going to take some possession from her yard in the dark of night, he said, "If you have to take it to bed with you every night, you don't own it. It owns you!"

The parsonage had been painted yellow in a previous lifetime, and it was time to give it another coat of paint. I talked to the elders about it in an elders meeting. I said that if the church would buy the paint, I would paint the house. I told them I would get yellow paint from Sears, and it was approved. Hugh thought it should be painted white. "Every house ought to be white. With white shingles."

Wes and I went to Sears in Wichita to get the yellow paint, and when we returned home, it was with a nice shade called Williamsburg Blue. She selected a burgundy color for the trim. The salesclerk showed us a brochure of a house painted in these colors, and the shingles that went with it were Desert Tan. It was striking!

A newcomer to the church had experience as a painter and was kind enough to help me scrape and paint the house. His other experience was with armed robbery. He had recently become a Christian after he had been released from prison due to his good behavior. That is, due to his good behavior after his bad behavior!

He told me a lot of things covered by the sanctity of the confessional, but one thing he told me was that he held the record in the state of Kansas for the most armed robberies in a single night. It was less than twenty. Barely. It was a drug-and-alcohol-fueled spree between

Hutchinson and Wichita. The Wichita police caught up with him in his hotel room sitting on the bed throwing money up in the air with both hands as he celebrated his *Guinness Book*-worthy achievement.

With his help, the work went fast. Another newcomer to the church was a contractor, and, with my help, he put on the new shingles—Desert Tan.

At the next elders meeting, Albert Wetmore smiled and commented that the paint color (Williamsburg Blue) was "an odd shade of yellow."

One of the things that gave Hugh delight was arguing with my wife. He thoroughly enjoyed provoking her, but to make up for it, he was always willing to share his opinions. One evening Wes and I were outside the parsonage with our two children, Nathaniel and Anna.[22] Anna was no more than a few months old. Hugh had something like the proverbial 8th grade education and no more, but he was one of the wisest men that I knew.

Hugh moved slowly down the alley beside the parsonage and turned off his big, rumbling Silverado. He slid out and dropped down to the ground. He had just closed the door when he shared with us his opinion. The way he held his hand looked something like God's in Michelangelo's depiction in the Sistine Chapel of the Creation of Adam. With the palm turned downward and the lax forefinger indicating our children, he said, "Them's your treasures." He then went on to expatiate upon his reasons that every couple, if able, should have at least

---

[22] Nathaniel and Anna were born in Ponca City, Oklahoma, while I pastored Tonkawa Bible Church. Our thirdborn, Caleb, was born in Ft. Dodge, Iowa.

three children. His statements were direct and a bit crude, but his thinking influenced me. We have three children, even though I was something of a product of the times in which I was schooled. The common thinking was "two and no more." I have passed along his counsel to other young couples on dozens of occasions with a nuanced explanation of his frank expression of his reasoning. The way Hugh put it was: "If you lose one, you have a spare." I have seen families in the throes of unimaginable pain and horrid grief at the loss of a child. Having other children to clutch to the breast and to share the burden helps only slightly.

Another of the things Hugh was adamant about was that children should grow up on a farm. Hugh and Oleita had three adult children who lived in the Tulsa area. One was an orthopedic surgeon, and the others were professionals in other fields. On a farm you learn to be creative with what you have—and all you need to fix anything is a little baling wire and a pair of pliers—well, almost anything. Sometimes you need duct tape! The creativity and ingenuity required by farm life are the bonuses added to the development of an invincible work ethic.

His ideas on the color of houses and roofs made sense in his world. Hugh and his sons owned thirty-five white rental houses and apartments. Keep a bundle of white shingles in your pickup along with a brush and a five-gallon bucket of white paint, and you are ready for much of the upkeep.

I remember one day in the middle of June when I bumped into Oleita. "Where's Hugh?"

"Oh, he's just like a little boy on Christmas morning! He's getting his combine ready for the wheat."

Oleita looked like Mrs. Santa Claus should look: she had a big smile with happy eyes and prominent ruby cheeks. She was a faithful worker in our little church, but she also was active in children's ministries in the community. One Saturday afternoon she called me in a panic. She had put together an event for a couple of dozen children. It was to take place in the shelter house in the park with the champion elm tree. Her speaker had canceled at the last minute. She wondered if I would fill in. The moment of the event arrived, and I rushed in to be introduced to the children by Oleita.

She began to offer the most memorable introduction I had in all my years of public speech: "As you children know, I had invited a gospel magician to come, and I know you boys and girls were looking forward to him, and you would have enjoyed him so much because he is so, so good. He is a magician and a clown and is just so much fun to listen to. He couldn't come, but this is Pastor Eddie."

Hugh and Oleita would hook up their camper trailer just after Christmas every year, and they would join the snowbird migration to South Texas. I always felt a little bit insecure whenever they would leave town. I suppose I had come to depend a great deal on Hugh, and Oleita was such a cheerful encouragement to both Wes and me.

The last time I saw Hugh was after he had lost his dear wife. It had been a dozen years since I had last returned to Tonkawa to speak at a church reunion. Hugh was seated in his front room in the home I had visited many times. A caregiver was attending. He was breathing oxygen through a nasal cannula, and the caregiver warned me that his memory was lapsing. As I sat down, I said, "Hugh, do you remember me?" He looked at me with a bit of expectancy but with no recognition. I continued, "I'm Eddie Brown. I was your pastor at Tonkawa Bible Church." It was obvious he did not remember me, but when I mentioned my name, he said with some relish: "His wife was a firecracker!"

Chapter Four

____

"God Uses Unlikely People"

I had been a pastor of a church for only a few days when I walked into the parsonage for lunch one day. I had traversed the fifty feet across the alley between the church and the parsonage. When I came through the kitchen, there was a woman on her knees. She was bent over at the waist with her face just inches from the floor. She was painting the baseboard. There was eighty-three-year-old Pearl Wetmore! Pearl Emma Sophiah Heldenbrand Wetmore!

"Pearl, what are you doing down there on your knees?" I said.

"I need to spend a lot more time on my knees, Pastor."

Here was another of the world's greatest . . . serving the Lord by serving others.

Pearl's late husband, E.M. Wetmore, and Joe Marshall had founded Tonkawa Bible Church in 1951.

Farmers of a prior generation knew the name Wetmore because of his invention of a farm implement called the grinder-mixer. People in Tonkawa referred to him as "Old Man Wetmore" or "Mr. Wetmore." One Sunday a group of Christians had a meeting to discuss the building of a church building. They took up a collection. In that one offering, they raised 15% of the proposed cost of the project. Mr. Wetmore quietly supplied the other 85%, and the lovely stone structure was built, complete with exquisite stained-glass windows.

More than anyone else, Pearl could provide for me a loving account of the backgrounds of each of my parishioners. From time to time she would accompany me to visit various widows in the outlying areas of Kay County.

Pearl lived in a modest home across the street from her sixty-four-year-old daughter, Myrtle, and two doors down from her fifty-nine-year-old son, Albert. Albert's wife, Doris, was the church organist. Pearl's granddaughter's family lived a few blocks to the north. There were four generations of her family in our little church.

Myrtle lived alone with her dog, Buddy, a gentle but somewhat decrepit black Labrador retriever. Buddy went with Myrtle everywhere, and if he lived today, he would have been a service dog. She drove an old powder blue Pontiac station wagon, and Buddy would lie contentedly on a pallet in the back.

Myrtle had in her home many of the leftover books from the Christian bookstore once owned and operated by her entrepreneurial father, Mr. Ernest Wetmore. She was anxious to share one of her books with me after the Sunday sermon of a similar topic, so on one of my visits, she urged me to take it home to read. Like many of us, she underlined the important words or phrases or paragraphs, but in Myrtle's estimation of this book, it was all important. Every word and line in the book were underlined with a red pencil. Of course, when everything is underlined, in effect, nothing is underlined.

Once every three months, a special visitor from Oklahoma City would arrive to stay with Myrtle. Kathleen Barkett was a Child Evangelism Fellowship missionary to rural Oklahoma schools. Kathleen would join Myrtle for a few days during which they went to some of the few remaining one-room schoolhouses in north-central Oklahoma. Kathleen was a spiritual giant despite being less than five feet tall. By the time I knew her she was very stooped and in her mid-eighties, so Myrtle would be her chauffer and Buddy their companion. Together they would share the message of Jesus with children in schools in rural places that weren't even on most maps. The teachers and the communities and the children welcomed them and celebrated their coming.

Like his father, Albert was creative with his hands. He was a wheat farmer as well as a machinist in the old Wetmore farm implement company that had been bought out by United Farm Tool. Albert's machinery was never the newest, and every year the harvest would present its challenges. There were times when the combine would break down early in the harvest. Albert would go to town to check the price on the part, and if the price was $400, it was too high! He would go to the machine shop and make the part for his combine. Frequently, his dismal and disheveled grey wheat was still standing late into the fall.

If Albert could be accused of pinching pennies in the wheat field, he was completely generous when it came to supporting the church. Once in an elders meeting, I made a proposal to take the church youth to Dallas to go to Six Flags Over Texas and to have a spiritual retreat featuring friends of mine in Arlington as the speakers. Albert reached into his back pocket and pulled out a $100 bill. He loved the youth and proved it.

After Anna, our second child, was born in May of 1982, we had a week's vacation coming in early July. With a two-month-old along with our two-year-old, we were penniless again, and we had planned to go camping in Arkansas around Eureka Springs on our way to see our parents in Mississippi. Albert heard about that and reached for his wallet after church that Sunday morning. He put $200 in my hand and told me to get a motel.

One Sunday morning, Pearl Wetmore was not in church. That was unusual because Pearl and her daughter, Myrtle, always came to church, unless Myrtle was sick. Even then, Pearl would catch a ride with Albert. But this Sunday Albert said that Pearl had not been well for about three days. That evening in church, still he was reluctant to say exactly what her problem was. When our resident nurse, Virginia, pressed him, he finally leaned over and whispered that she was constipated. Because of the nature of the problem, he had described her condition inexactly as "not feeling well."

By the evening service at church Pearl was worse. Her breath had a foul odor, Albert said. Nurse Virginia said, "Albert, get her to the hospital immediately!" So at 8:45, the ambulance sped toward the hospital in Ponca City, Oklahoma.

The next morning the family and I were at her bedside. The surgeon said her bowel was impacted. He suspected that she had a twisted bowel. She was in her early eighties then, and the surgeon said that because she had waited so long to come in, her chances of living through the surgery were not good. As we gathered around her for prayer, she said to me: "Pastor, have you met my son, Albert?" We prayed and committed her care to the physicians and to her Heavenly Father.

She survived the surgery, but her condition was not improving. She developed pneumonia. Within a few days her doctor went out of town to a convention. While he was gone, the nurses failed to give her the proper medication for 3 days. Her condition declined. Pearl's granddaughter was a nurse and had come home from Guatemala where she was a missionary. She sneaked a peek at the hospital charts and discovered that the nurses had not followed the doctor's orders properly. Pearl was again very near death. The family was called in. She wouldn't last the day, we were told.

All the while I wondered what would happen to our little church when this frail little spiritual giant should go to be with the Lord. "What's going to happen to the church, Lord?" Her presence held her family and the church together. If we lost her, our little church might be splintered in the crash.

What no one expected came about.[23] Pearl was released from the hospital. For a month she lay in bed—a virtual invalid needing help for everything she did.

"Why did God keep me alive? What good am I to anyone? Nobody needs this old woman." These are things she would say. "What can an old woman do for the Lord?" I've heard the same sentiments expressed over the years so frequently from widows who survive their husbands and live lives they think to be too long.

If we live long enough, virtually all of us will one day have a period of depression. Obviously, it is deeper and more severe for some than for others, and for some it becomes a way of life. Pearl was soon back to her usual encouraging self, blessing others and even teaching the children's Sunday School class she had taught in the same room for thirty-five years.

The Scriptures show over and over that God can use people you wouldn't expect. The Lord can use unlikely people like you and me.[24]

After our first few months in Tonkawa, one spring night Wes and I heard the sound of an ambulance moving through town. We could tell that the siren had come down

---

[23] We were like the disciples in the Early Church. In Acts 12, a young woman named Rhoda answered the door and saw an answer to the prayers of the Christians in Jerusalem. She ran to tell the disciples, and they disbelieved that the Lord had answered their prayer. We had prayed, but we were amazed that Pearl recovered. The Lord is good.

[24] Moses claimed he was a nobody and not eloquent (Ex. 3:11, 4:10); Gideon objected that his family was poor and that he was too young (Judg. 6:15); Jeremiah reprised the claims of lacking eloquence and of being too young (Jer. 1:6); but Isaiah said: "Here am I; send me" (Isa. 6:8 AV).

Grand and that the ambulance had turned north on a street to the west of us.

The next morning Pearl called to tell me that Wanda Gillispie had been taken by ambulance to the hospital about eight miles north of Tonkawa to the bigger, little town of Blackwell where the nearest hospital was. The Blackwell Hospital was about the size of most Hampton Inns—about three stories high and not too long. I would stop at the desk, and then walk up the stairs to Wanda's room.

My first visit to Wanda was very likely my second hospital visit as a pastor.

I had met Wanda and Lawrence at church. He was short and pleasant and quiet, and she was short and pleasant and fluffy. I had seen them in church a few times, but when I got to the hospital, she was in a semi-private room. In that room I discovered two ladies with a curtain divider on an overhead track. When I walked in, both of them were lying down—and, truth be known, both of them were probably snoring.

There was no name on a white board above the bed as you often see today. I couldn't tell which of the early-seventies ladies was Wanda. Some of my younger readers don't know this yet, but when old people lie down, their face comes down toward the pillow. I mean, their face doesn't cover their ears, usually, but with the pillow rising up and their face flowing down, it gives the same basic effect. And of course, their glasses are off. And, if they are removable, their teeth are out. That's what's in the glass on the nightstand, like a frog in formaldehyde.

My point is that when older people lie down, their faces do too. They become unrecognizable to people who haven't known them very long. And I had met Wanda just a couple of times as she exited church after one of my delightful sermons, full of helpful substance and just the right length.

I walked back and forth between the two beds trying to see some sign of which one was Wanda, and finally, one of them stirred and said, "Pastor Eddie."

"Whew."

Wanda sat up, and I said, "Well, Wanda. You're looking good."

She didn't miss a beat. "Don't tell me I'm looking good! Tell me I'm good-looking."

Wanda had angina. She regularly would have chest pains, but sometimes they just would not quit. Lawrence would call for the ambulance, and the ambulance would roar over to their house. The EMTs would go in with the stretcher. The first few times it happened, the neighbors would come out to see what was going on, but they pretty soon figured out that it was just Wanda having chest pains again. Every three months or so this scene would be repeated. If we listened carefully, we could tell that the siren would stop about slightly north of us and about 2 blocks away from the church parsonage on 1st Street. It would stop at Wanda's house. And Pearl would let me know the following day. Pearl was everyone's grandma.

Chapter Five

"A Gift from God and a
Few New Friends"

Our first year in Tonkawa was very eventful. The summer brought temperatures that were record-breaking. We had 100 days that summer in which the temperature was 100 degrees or higher, and 45 days in a row it was that extreme! I remember seeing the thermometer outside one of the town banks that read 114°. Many nights at 10:00 PM the temperature was still a blistering 95 degrees.

Around my October birthday Wes was expecting our first child. She had suffered a miscarriage the October before, so this pregnancy was one of concern and consolation.

On that terrible night of the miscarriage Wes had awakened me around 2:00 AM to tell me the horrid news. The verse of comfort that the Lord brought to my mind that night was Psalm 34:19. "Many are the afflictions of the righteous, but the Lord delivers him out of them all" (NASB). I understood that Christians are not exempt from troubles but that the Lord would see us through. We wept. We prayed and comforted one another, and the Lord comforted us.

Finally, the day of the birth of our firstborn arrived, and in my journal, I recorded these words concerning Monday, October 12, 1980.

> Yesterday was one of the most amazing days of my life. It ranks with the date of my trusting in Christ, marrying my wife, and being ordained. Yesterday, Nathaniel Edward Joseph Brown was born. It was with praiseful awe that I witnessed my wife give birth to life. Not prone to expressing [publicly] my praise for God, it was difficult to stifle words of praise and thanksgiving. It was one of the several most worshipful times of my life. Now Lord, will you save him and cause him to grow up loving you? Will you make him a man in whom there is no guile?[25]

The next concern was how to pay for him. Wes and I had saved some $1,100 while we both worked the few months following seminary before we had been led to the ministry in Tonkawa. We hadn't earned much then, but it was two hundred dollars more a month than I was receiving as the pastor of a tiny church. Our savings could pay only a portion of the bill. We owed nearly $1,800 to the hospital and to the doctor for the birth of our son.

---

[25] When Jesus was calling His disciples and challenging them to follow Him, He declared of Nathanael, ". . . Behold an Israelite indeed, in whom is no guile" (John 1:47 AV). Nathanael was one who spoke his mind and did not seek to deceive others with hypocritical fawning.

Dear friends who knew something of our situation sent $500. I was helping a contractor in our church with roofing jobs and concrete work to help cover our expenses. By God's grace, we had just what we needed.

Before Nathaniel was born, Wes and I had enrolled in childbirth classes at the hospital where he was to be born. There in Ponca City we met a young couple who were to have a child within two weeks of ours. Like us, they had recently moved to the area for work. Dennis Coates worked at Conoco, and Donna was training to be a nurse. They lived a few miles west of Tonkawa, and we began to visit back and forth.

About the same time, we were getting to know our neighbors, Larry and Reta Swords, and we had met John and Debbie Birch. All had children about the age of ours, and they became the ones who brought their children to our birthday parties, and we took ours to theirs. They were the friends with whom we went out to eat, on special occasions, and Larry and Reta graciously took us out to the lake. Larry contends that he taught half of Tonkawa how to ski.

At some point Dennis went back to college. That brought him to my house periodically so I could help him with his English for Freshman Composition. Dennis took me on my first quail hunt. We walked all over his quarter of a section of land and saw no quail. We stopped back at his house briefly, and Dennis was inside when I saw a covey of quail come out of the barn, not fifty feet from me. He had assumed too much, and Dennis had not informed me that it was not kosher to shoot at the quail while they were on the ground, since that would not be sporting. No matter. I didn't hit them anyway. BLAM! BLAM! BLAM! Off they flew. Yes, it was a shotgun, and, yes, I really did miss them.

Before I played golf a few times a year, I played tennis a few times a year, and when I did, I played with John Birch, the president of one of the local banks. We were pretty evenly matched, neither of us being ranked very high in the professional standings. Our wives and children would visit when we played on the college tennis courts a couple of blocks from his house.

Summer came again, and so did the opportunity for vacation. Vacations meant camping on the way to see family. On this particular occasion we loaded up the car on Sunday night and took three-and-one-half-year-old Nathaniel and two-year-old Anna to the car at 4:00 AM. Our plan was to camp in southeastern Indiana on the way to see my sister in central Kentucky. We would camp on the banks of the Blue River. I had three weeks of vacation saved for the visit with my sister and the subsequent trip to Mississippi to see our parents.

It was almost impossible to fall asleep when we were planning to leave so early, but on June 25, 1984, we piled our little toddlers into their car seats and took off well before sunup. Wes went back to sleep so she could drive at 6:00 AM, the time when I always fell asleep on such trips.

We drove for a thousand hours with two kids under four years old. Our campsite was near Milltown, Indiana, and it was about 45 minutes from Louisville, Kentucky. Wes had stopped the car on the hillside toward the river. (It's not important to note who had parked the car on the hill or who had failed to set the emergency brake!) The week before we left, I had gone to the Western Auto Store and had purchased battery-operated toy trucks for Nathaniel and Anna. That gave them something to do while we set up camp. We were unpacking the luggage carrier on top of our car so we could set up our tent on the hillside above the Blue River.

Suddenly Wes screamed! When I turned around, I saw our 1979 Datsun station wagon—our "little red wagon"—gaining speed and beginning to gallop toward the river. Had Nathaniel just been inside the car? Had he knocked the car out of gear? I looked quickly to see that the kids were out of the way. The front door on the passenger's side flew open. The window was down, and I grabbed the door frame as it rolled past. I reasoned that I could push the car, so perhaps I could stop the car! The car jerked me forward and slammed me against the rear door. I let go, but the car kept going, gathering speed downhill. I had just had a cyst removed from my left elbow. The stitches had not held, and I was bleeding again.

We watched helplessly as the car rolled forty feet down the slight hill until it got to the last 12 feet to the river. The car lunged forward down the forty-five-degree grade. It crashed into a tree just as its front bumper sunk into the water. Anna and Nathaniel burst into tears. Wes and I were in shock.

Everything in the open luggage carrier slid out and into the water. Did you know that Coleman lanterns and camp stoves don't float? But it would have been a great commercial for old-timey Samsonite luggage. Our two suitcases, our clothes bag with my new suit, and our sleeping bags went floating down the river. I am a poor swimmer, so I was going to let everything float away to the Gulf of Mexico.

Our little red wagon

Between me and the river was 12 feet of poison ivy! I hate poison ivy and am severely allergic to it. Thankfully (I suppose!), a dozen college students were playing volleyball a short distance away. They heard the crash and came running. Within a few minutes I was wading barefoot through the 12-inch-high poison ivy to retrieve our luggage when the college kids brought it to the riverbank.

With everything crushed or wet, we had to spend $45 on a night in a motel. For $20 we rented a pickup for a day.

My sister, Jeannie, lived four hours away in Somerset, Kentucky. She picked us up the next afternoon, and she and my family dropped me off at the Louisville airport. I was the last person to board the plane, and seconds later they closed the door behind me. The one-way ticket cost over $317. Our vacation money was all gone. I flew back to Tulsa to get our other car to continue our trip.

Before I went to college, I had thought of becoming a pharmacist. I had plenty of time to reflect on other directions my life might have taken. It seemed that my life had begun to revolve around money—never having enough of it to do anything but just barely get the bills paid, and often that was through the charity of others. After my third year of college, I had a job offer that came with a $25,000 salary. One bachelor's degree, one master's degree, and eight years after that offer, I was making $1200 a month, barely half of that offer.

When I had called my insurance agent, Guy Lyall, he volunteered to drive our other car to meet me at the Tulsa airport. Hugh Simmons got him into the parsonage for the car keys, and Guy and his wife graciously drove from Tonkawa to the Tulsa airport, 110 miles, one-way. After thanking them heartily, I drove through the night to my sister's home in Somerset, Kentucky.

When I got there, all our vacation money was spent, and I had purchased gas with our credit card! Our good car was totaled; and my poison ivy had just begun to itch.

I was not happy.

I know. I hadn't lost much. It was of a material nature. It was replaceable. But I was still having to deal with the disappointment and inconvenience and financial loss of hundreds of dollars when we had very little. To make it just a little bit worse, I had just put a brand-new tire on the car to make the trip a little safer. I was angry and resentful and grieving. I am a real person, and this is how real people feel.

And if all that wasn't enough, the Lord wouldn't leave me alone. He was urging me to deal with my bad attitude.

We spent a few days with my sister and then got in the car to go to our parents' homes in Mississippi. As is our custom, when we leave in the car from home, we pray together. Wes was driving, and I began to look in the glove compartment to see if I could find a New Testament. I found instead a little booklet of Bible verses entitled "Precious Bible Promises." I opened the booklet to a page which said: "In everything give thanks, for this is the will of God in Christ Jesus concerning you."[26]

---

[26] 1 Thess. 5:18 (AV).

I felt like Jonah when the Lord said to him, "Do you do well to be angry?"[27]

"Yes!" Jonah said. "I have good reason to be angry!"

But Jonah didn't, and I didn't either.

Finally, as we continued on our trip, I prayed aloud with Wes and I said, "Lord, I come to you, and you've told me to give thanks in everything. I'm coming in the midst of our situation, and I want to give you thanks."

Please notice the crucial distinction: I did not give thanks *FOR* everything but *IN* everything! In every situation and at all times, give thanks to the Lord. Look for things for which you should give thanks. There is a submission to the Lord as sovereign that brings about humility before His greatness—a humility which enables one to pray and give thanks to the loving greatness that is the Lord of our salvation.

At the time, I made a list of the things for which I should give thanks to the Lord.

1. Our children had been in the car just moments before the car rolled to the river.
2. Anna's toy car had been crushed by our car as it rolled to the river. She had just been where the car rolled.
3. The car hit a big tree in the water's edge, and the front bumper was the only part of the car in the water. That saved my briefcase and my Bible.
4. The Lord proved Romans 8:28 to me. With the insurance money (and a loan from my banker friend, John Birch) I replaced our five-year-old car with 80,000 miles on it with a three-year-old Subaru wagon with 27,000 miles on it.

---

[27] Jon. 4:4, 9 (NASB).

In those dark days I found things for which to be thankful while in the midst of difficulty. Sadly, I must say that I have learned, and I have had to relearn many times that a thankful heart rejoices in and rests in a faithful Father.

We had been back at home in Tonkawa for a few days when I ran into Jack, a pastor friend, who greeted me jauntily: "I heard you had a smashing vacation."

Chapter Six

"Christmas and The Newlyweds"

Our first Christmas in Tonkawa was upon us. Somewhere I found a free cedar tree, and we decorated it with our small collection of antique Christmas tree ornaments and twinkling lights.

In celebration of our first Christmas in Tonkawa, Wes the Entertainer decided to invite the four elders and their wives for snacks and games. The game she decided on was "The Newlyweds." Among the elders, the "newliest" of the newlyweds, after us, were wed some 45 years before. The others had been married 48, 50, and 60 years before!

In the game, the couple was separated. The wives went out of the room, and the husbands were questioned. We wrote down their answers. When the wives returned, we asked them the same questions to see how each wife would answer. When the wives answered, the typical response of the husbands was something like, "Well, that's not how it happened at all!" or "What were you thinking? What about the time we . . . ."

One of the questions was: "What was the best gift he ever gave you?"

Joe Marshall was born in 1902 and was 78 years old at this Christmas party. "What was the best gift you ever gave Mabel?" "Well, it was the only gift I ever gave her. It was a 1971 Plymouth, Royal Blue and White." It seems that he had bought it and driven it home as a surprise. He went inside: "Happy Birthday! I have a surprise for you." He covered her eyes and led her outside. He said, "Keep your eyes closed." He took off the blindfold. "Open your eyes."

"It's the wrong color," she said, and she went back inside.

Oddly, that was the only gift he ever bought her.

One summer day in 1984, Joe said he was thinking of doing something he had always wanted to do and had never done. He wanted to take his ancient and heavy, wooden johnboat out west of town to a public access point on the Salt Fork River. From there he wanted to paddle and float down the river to a takeout point at the edge of town. Of course, as an 82-year-old man, he couldn't do it alone. He wanted to go on Monday, the Fourth of July. I said I would go with him.

The morning came and I went to help Joe load the boat in the trunk of the huge old wrong-colored, blue and white Plymouth. Mabel was driving us, and we went across the river on the south side of town and turned west on Fountain Road. I asked Joe and Mabel if we could go to a home just west of the interstate highway. I had been told it was a mile west of the interstate and a mile south of Fountain Road.

On the Saturday before, I had been washing my little red Datsun 210 station wagon in the front yard of the parsonage. A car had parked alongside the church, and out of it popped a man in his mid-fifties. He had a huge smile on his face and a jaunty air. He strode up confidently like an old friend on whom I had been waiting expectantly. He said loudly as he approached: "Ahhhh, Pastor! Good to see you! I told you I would be back!"

I looked at him and smiled because that's what one does to someone speaking so familiarly and jovially, and he had just about convinced me that he knew me and that I could not quite remember him. He knew my name, but it is not terribly difficult to find out the name of a pastor in a small town.

I said to him, "I don't think we have ever met."

"Oh, of course we have, Pastor! We visited here a couple of months ago, and I told you we were moving here."

I was still shaking my head, and I was certain we had not met. In a church with 50 people in the pews on a good Sunday, I noticed EVERY visitor we had. What's more, in those days when my mind had some elasticity and acuity, I remembered every visitor. And their names! I had not seen this Irish-seeming, hail-fellow-well-met. Ever!

But confidence men (and women) have a way about them, and so did this gentleman. "Pastor, we'll be in church tomorrow, and you'll remember my daughter. She had polio, and she walks with a limp. Pastor, here's our situation. We bought the old Johnson place a mile west of the interstate and a mile south of Fountain Road. Do you know it?"

"No, I can't say that I do."

"Well, here's the deal. The moving van is thirty miles south in Perry at a truck stop, and they won't unload our things until we pay the final $300. I have $260 on me, and the problem is that my wallet is in the glove box of my car, and my car is on the moving van. I need $40 so they will unload. Pastor, I can pay you back tomorrow at church."

As you read these words, you must notice that his story had enough details to make it believable. It had verisimilitude—the semblance of truth. But I didn't have $40. At that time $40 was an astronomical amount to me. Our savings were gone. I had $20 and enough for some groceries and some gas for our car.

I called Hugh Simmons. As a successful farmer and real estate investor, Hugh could spare $40. He was not at home. I called Joe Marshall at the Western Auto Store. I told Joe that I would give the man $20 if he would. He said that he would. I took our $20 from our safe place and led the charming man to the Western Auto Store. He said again that he would pay us back the next day.

Something must have come up because he and his wife and his daughter who limped severely were not in church the next day.

Monday was the Fourth of July. Mabel was driving her blue and white Plymouth with the boat hanging way out of the trunk. I asked her to turn south one mile west of the interstate. We went the one mile, and there was the old house on the corner. It was the house the charming gentleman had called "the old Johnson place." It was partially shaded by dust-covered, dried-up elm trees with limbs long since broken in Oklahoma thunderstorms. Weeds were sticking up out of the broken floorboards of the front porch.

There was no moving van there. I did think I saw the tumbleweed I had seen on our first visit to Tonkawa. Joe smiled, and my jaw dropped just a little. The charmer was not the only confidence man ever to inveigle some cash from me, but he was certainly the best.

The boat went into the water with a bit of a splash and a bit of a thud. The heavy boat sank deep enough that I wondered at the wisdom of the undertaking, but we were committed. Joe made his way to the back of the boat, and I sank my Converse All-Star Chuck Taylors into the deep, black silty mud and pushed us out of the shallows into the deep waters of the Salt Fork River. It must have been five feet deep in places

Some five hours later we stepped ashore in the mud alongside of the river. Five hours was a long time in the hot Oklahoma summer sun, but it was a well-invested time spent with a worthy man like Joe Marshall.

When the summer was ending and the leaves on the walnut trees were beginning to turn yellow, Joe asked what I thought about having a Sunday picnic in early October. We could have our evening service in the late afternoon before coming home, he suggested.

The plan was to leave together after Sunday morning worship and caravan the 45 miles to the Newkirk area near where Joe had grown up. We would have a picnic on the Buffalo Bluffs of the Arkansas River. It was there that

Native Americans had stampeded bison over the 15-foot cliff. By stampeding them over the cliff they conserved their arrows.

Joe said he knew just the place. All we needed to do was to drive over one afternoon and get the permission of the farmer who owned the land. Didn't he have a telephone? Why, of course he did.

One Friday afternoon Mabel tended the Western Auto store, and around two o'clock Joe and I got into his little Chevrolet pickup ready for a road trip. He putted along at about 45 miles per hour, and we arrived in just about an hour. We got to the area and went directly to the spot Joe had in mind for the picnic. There in the shade above the bluffs were two six-foot-long bull snakes. I picked one of them up and was amazed at how docile it was. It seemed as though they were a mating pair and that they had lived in that area undisturbed for all of their lives. When I put it down, it went into a hole under a large oak. A year later when we were on the same scouting trip prior to our picnic and service at the Buffalo Bluffs, I found the same two snakes, still as unperturbed by our presence as before.

We never saw the farmer, so I at first surmised that Joe had called him on the telephone to get his permission. No, he had not called. Joe had just wanted an outing to explore the trails of his youth. So had I.

The Sunday of the picnic finally came, and the preacher had a shorter sermon than usual. There were not more than 30 of my parishioners on the picnic, but the older folk sat and visited, and the half a dozen younger ones climbed on rocks and walked in the almost-dry riverbed. Doris Wetmore found some beautiful, bright red plants with many leaves on each stem. She picked an armful for decorating back at home. Albert informed her that the beautiful plant was poison sumac. And, yes, she later regretted picking them.

When it came time for our evening service, lawn chairs came out of car trunks and were arranged near the bluff where I would speak. We needed more chairs.

Wes said to me abruptly: "Brown Eddie, go get our chairs out of the back of the car."

I turned to go, and Steve Rench, a young engineer who was my age, announced loudly to the crowd, "Boy, is he hen-pecked!"

To which Wes immediately replied, "Brown Eddie, tell him you're not hen-pecked!"

"I'm not hen-pecked!" I retorted quickly in mock sheepishness.

Of course I understood the logical ramifications of my answer. If I followed her instructions to say I wasn't hen-pecked, it proved that I was. Hmmm! All in good fun.

One evening Joe called me to tell me that two great horned owls had perched in the southeast part of town. He came by in his little pickup, and we drove the five blocks to the area. He slowly came to a stop, and then we crept just as slowly to get near enough to observe them through his binoculars. They are to this day the only ones I have ever seen. The following morning at daybreak, they were perched across the street from the parsonage in a tree by the home of Larry Swords. Nathaniel was only two years old, but I woke him up to join me on the front porch to see them. It did not make a great impression on him. He rubbed his eyes and soon fell asleep again.

Joe shared my love of trees as well. On one occasion he picked me up to go to see a blue heron nest on the Chikaskia River east of town. The nest was in a sycamore tree that Joe knew. Actually, two sycamores had grown up inches apart, and both had been undisturbed for the better part of a century. Each had a 17-foot girth. Joe had measured them.

On one of our trips Joe talked to me about his funeral. Over the years, many of my parishioners have done the same. Joe said that he didn't want any eulogy. He just wanted the Lord to be glorified. "Now promise me that you won't do a long eulogy."

I said to him: "Joe, when you're gone, I'll do what I want!"

You can imagine that I was planning quite a eulogy. Some months later we moved to northern Iowa when I became the pastor of another church. I was not present at his funeral. This is my eulogy of Joe Marshall.

Chapter Seven

"The Lady in Lavender"

After our move to Missouri, my oddities and eccentricities had been on full display one Sunday while I preached. I admit to being somewhat obsessive-compulsive in nature, but I always contended to my parishioners that I am OCD in a charming sort of way. Such things are easily noticed.

In the days when I preached regularly, I would get to the pulpit at the time for the sermon to begin. Before I uttered a word, I would obsessively clear off the top level of the pulpit and would almost always remove a hymn book, paper programs of the day's events and announcements, and the little three-inch golf cart pencils available in the back of the pews for signing our attendance books, and, quite frequently, the odd paper clip or plastic top of a cheap Bic pen.

When those items were removed, then I would be able

to turn my attention to more important things, like making sure the pulpit itself was perfectly perpendicular to the center aisle and making sure the pulpit was centered on the imaginary line from the clock on the wall at the other end of the center aisle. When those crucial things were accomplished, then I would be able to remove my sermon manuscript from my Bible and place it on the top level of the pulpit beside my Bible which would be opened to the passage from which I planned to preach.

One Sunday, Rita White commented after the sermon that she had thought of a television show that I might like. She knew that we did not have cable or the capability of watching broadcast television and that we had chosen not to have a satellite television system. Rita said, "The character on the show reminds me of you." The show she mentioned was *Frasier*. I'm sure it was his urbane sophistication and not his fussy, obsessive-compulsivity that made her think of me.

My earlier mention of painstakingly producing an actual printed-by-hand manuscript of each sermon may have given the perceptive reader a peep into the depths of my personality and my compulsive tendencies.

After a few months in Tonkawa, the church service had gotten underway. The invocation had been offered, and a couple of hymns had been sung when I realized I had left my sermon manuscript on the couch in the parsonage, just across the alley from the church. During the last hymn before the message, I abruptly left the front pew where I had been perched in preparation for preaching. I exited to my left and went out the door of the small chapel that was on the east side of the church.

There on the sidewalk about to enter the front door was the "lady in lavender." I had seen her a number of times in our services. A lady in a lavender dress—always in the same lavender dress—would sit every week on the row at the back on the left side. She would always arrive during the hymns and would always leave during the closing prayer. Once I had called on someone to offer the benedictory prayer, and I rushed to the back of the church to block her exit so I could meet her and solve the mystery of her identity. I failed. She had already escaped!

Hugh Simmons was over one day. I asked him who the "lady in lavender" was.

"Oh, that's Faye Phillips," Hugh said.

"Well, I've been trying to meet her."

"Good luck," was all he said. She was notorious for arriving late and leaving early so as to avoid conversation with others at church.

So there I was, in the providence of the Lord and due to my forgetfulness and OCDness, finally, face-to-face with the "lady in lavender." I said, "Hi! I'm Eddie Brown."

She replied, "I'm Faye Phillips. I've been wanting to meet you. Actually, I didn't want to meet you. I wanted to get to know you first!" She had observed me for some months and was beginning to sense that I might not be too much of a threat nor too unpleasant.

The following week I went to her home for a visit. Her house was a common style in Tonkawa. It had a front porch with a three-foot brick wall holding up fat-based columns perched on the wall. The front porch was covered by the overhang of the front portion of the second story in the "Craftsman" style. She owned the lot to the south of her as well. Her yard seemed decorated with various ornaments and farm implements and other steel objects of varying sizes. It would have been a nightmare to mow.

She warmly invited me into her living room where we had an enjoyable visit. She explained to me the mystery of her late arrivals and early departures. It seems that someone, at some time, said that she had talked too long after church and had held him or her up. Her response was never to talk to anyone at church again.

Like many of us, she could not be persuaded to give people another chance. She was quite implacable. After an hour or so, I was preparing to leave. Faye said she wanted to pray for me. I sat on her couch and began to bow my head for prayer. I wasn't prepared for what happened next. She knelt beside her chair and propped her elbows up in the chair. She rested her folded hands against her forehead, and she began to pray. She prayed a sincere and heartfelt prayer for "her pastor" and his family. She had gotten to know me, so she was ready to meet me.

As long as I was in the church, Faye would not be the only peculiar person with odd ways. Nor would I be! And then one Friday night, I met Ann Williams.

Wes and I had been in Tonkawa a few months when we planned to invite Dr. Ken Sheppard[28] to speak at our little church. Ken was the pastor who had presided over our wedding ceremony. I had gotten to know Ken in the first month of my time in college. He had pastored

---

[28] Ken Sheppard was the pastor of our home church in Jackson, Mississippi. Billie, his wife, and Ken live in the Dallas area. Ken has been my friend and my pastor since 1969.

Riverwood Bible Church in Jackson, Mississippi. I had done an internship under him after my third year of seminary.

Ken and Billie and their two children arrived one Friday in May of 1980 for a weekend Bible conference on the topic of Bible Prophecy. I had advertised the event in the local paper, naming the series "What in the World Is Going On?" We had a few visitors that first Friday night, but none so memorable as Ann Williams.

Before the service began, I went back to the pew where she was seated. I introduced myself and heard her and her husband's names: Ann and Roy Williams. The Williams lived up the road in Blackwell. Sitting beside Ann was a quiet man—a man who was never quite able to utter a word, considering the barrage of words his wife belched into the air. As unpleasant as Ann could be, he was pleasant. Ann had granny glasses perched on her nose, and her hair fled back from her forehead and face, racing to make a tight bun.

Ann began the interrogation: "What's your wife's name?"

"Wesley," I replied.

To which she demanded: "Wesley! What kind of name is that for a girl?"

From her gruff tone I surmised she was not seeking information but was expressing her disapproval of Wes's parents' choice of a name for their daughter, despite their Methodist heritage and their desire to honor an uncle as well as the founder of the Methodist Church.

Ann then immediately asked where I had gone to school.

"Dallas Theological Seminary," I said. She pressed for more information.

"What's your specialty?"

I was beginning to feel a bit off balance in answering her aggressive and probing queries. "Well, I really don't have a specialty," I replied, trying to smile my way out of the conversation. "I'm more of a GP kind of guy." I was trying to present myself as a general practitioner rather than a specialist in any biblical or theological field. I have always been a generalist in my approach to studies, and I have a wide range of interests in learning to this day.

None of my answers satisfied this demanding woman, and I quickly offered some reason for my escape so I could go on to meet other visitors. I would not be honest if I did not admit that pastors sometimes hope some visitors to their churches go on to find a church more to their liking. As delightful as Roy Williams was, before I really got to know her, Ann Williams made me want to help her find another church.

One reality in life is that not everyone gets along with everyone else. Another reality in life is that a pastor often has good instincts about people and how they will, or will not, fit with the flock that the pastor shepherds.

During my early months we saw the return of some of the people who had left the church during the tenure of the divisive pastor who had preceded me. One of those couples was also from Blackwell. We had come to enjoy visiting with Vernon and Twila Harris, and they had invited us to Sunday lunch on a couple of occasions.

Both had sweet spirits. They were well-established in their sixties, and Vernon's white hair was swept back from a widow's peak to a broad, thinly covered strip on the top of his head, and his light complexion was always blushing from its exposure to the sun. Twila had a bright smile, plump and rosy cheeks, and ginger hair with faint white streaks. Twila was the ultimate homemaker: a brilliant cook and an expert at canning her produce each year.

On our first visit to their home, Twila and Wes were inside putting the final touches on the lunch before Vernon and I were summoned from outside. Vernon and I were walking around their yard. They had a neat garden with the early promise of abundant vegetables to go along with the fruit from the many trees that shaded their backyard—pecan, apple, apricot, pear, and peach trees. In their garden were blueberries and strawberries, and at the edge of the yard were blackberries and raspberries.

Vernon drove a truck for an oil company. He would visit the various leases where there were wells and receiving tanks around northern Oklahoma. From those tanks he would pump the crude oil into a tanker to be taken to larger storage tanks before the oil was trucked to the refinery in Ponca City. When Vernon would come to the monthly elders meetings, Twila would come to visit Wes. They talked of childbirth and childrearing, of gardening and canning, of joys and of sorrows and of the disappointments of life. Twila was a mentor to Wes.

Twila once challenged her that our children didn't really take our words seriously. "You're just playing with them, and they know it!" The challenge involved the need to be firm and to follow up on the directives we gave to our children. Twila was from a large family and was born at a time when the infant mortality rates were high. She had several siblings who lived less than two years, and her mother had suffered multiple late-term miscarriages. Twila explained that she had grown up in a time and place in which parents did not count on their children's survival until they had weathered a few major childhood illnesses as well as pneumonia. Twila's mother had three stillborn babies before she had the seven who survived. My own grandmother used to say that when one had contracted pneumonia three times, it was usually fatal.

On a few occasions Vernon and Twila would take us out to eat on Sundays following Sunday morning services. They were becoming, with our parents six hundred and fifty miles away, something of surrogate, parental figures in our lives. Going out to eat on Sundays in Tonkawa meant going to eat in the college dining hall. One Sunday, after Ann and Roy Williams had begun to attend church regularly, we were forced to sit at the table with Ann Williams. Her conversation was loud and, I thought, offensive. She talked about Christian things—ideas I shared, but she spoke of them in tones that drew sidelong glances from others around us. Other conversations were hushed as her words trumpeted through the lunchroom. I was relieved to get back into the back seat of Vernon's car. Moments later we were in the alley behind the church and beside the parsonage. As I got out of the car, Twila offered this summation of our experience with Ann: "Don't you just love Ann!" I had what must have been an incredulous look on my face, and I cannot imagine that I found anything to say in reply.

It has always been my practice to visit those who visited the church, and it was time to visit the Williams in their home. I knocked on the door of the front porch. It was a screen door covered in translucent plastic to keep out the cold, winter winds. It had a few tears in it, but it shielded from view the stacks of magazines and the filing cabinets on the enclosed front porch. From there I was invited into their living room. The light was poor, and it seemed dusty enough that it was a little difficult to breathe. Ann was overjoyed to see me, and she launched into a historical disquisition detailing her ministry in the neighborhood over the years. I learned that for the prior twenty-five years, Ann and quiet Roy Williams had hosted a children's ministry in their home. On the walls were the trophies of that ministry. Large, framed pictures of twenty or more children from each year of ministry lined the upper reaches of the walls. In spite of her lack of ability to speak to and engage with adults, she was able to speak to children and to teach them from the Bible, and she had won many of them to a genuine faith in Jesus Christ.

She began to show me pictures of her various years of children's backyard Bible clubs, and she boasted that she could show me such albums for hours and hours, but after two hours I thought I had a general appreciation for the significance of her ministry and the pictorial record of it. It was, truly, significant. Quiet Roy ministered and helped in the background, and Ann spoke up forcefully, yet engagingly. She taught the children the Bible and the ways of Christ. I could not love her as Twila did, but my respect for her had grown significantly.

One day after church, Hugh Simmons and I were visiting in the little courtyard area just outside the chapel door. Ann appeared and hijacked the conversation. She threw out the challenge to me: "Pastor, how much do you think I weigh?"

I blushed and stammered sheepishly, "Well, Ann, I don't know!"

"Hugh, how about you? What do you think I weigh? Feel how solid my thigh is! It's pure muscle."

Hugh was an old farmer, and he could guess the weight of cattle within 50 pounds any old time, and there was nothing shy or diffident about him. "Oh, I'd say about a hundred and eighty-five pounds." He must have been about right because that was the end of the conversation. I think Ann expected a lower number so she could explain why the estimate was wrong because of her densely packed muscles. Hugh robbed her of that joy with a spot-on guess.

On other trips to Blackwell I went to visit Roy where he worked as a car detailer on the used cars acquired by one car dealership in town. Since he worked alone in a metal building in back of the dealership, I was able to visit him while he worked. He was a sweet man with a shaky, halting voice that vibrated in his throat and came out with a volume that rose and fell. I was always reminded of Mr. Haney on the old television show, *Green Acres.* When I was alone with Roy, he was both interesting and interested. Every conversation was through smiles and joy.

Once Roy told me of a time as a young teen when he had attended a wake when one of his young friends had died. He and a few friends were alone in the parlor of the home of the deceased. In the wee hours after the clock had struck one, the boys had become spooked by the breezes rippling the chiffon curtains, because at that exact moment, there was some inexplicable sound. They would have been at ease if not for the types of tales that had filled their conversations and now furnished their ready imaginations. Just then, one and then another noticed under the shroud that covered the corpse, there was, very definitely, movement. The hair on Roy's neck stood on end, and his eyes bulged with terror! He was unable to scream. The shroud still moved, and they knew the corpse was coming back to life. The family cat meowed and found her way out from under the shroud. The only sound the boys could make was a loud gasp.

On occasion, one of the sons of one of my parishioners would drive down from Wichita on a Sunday morning. His hair was coiffed and sprayed, and no hair dared stray from its assigned place. The dark, pin-striped suit, the expensive, white Pinpoint Oxford shirt beneath a perfectly matched silk tie, all combined to make him look like he had just left his high-rise office in his C.P.A. firm. He was a leader in his fundamentalist Baptist church in the big city, and his stentorian voice boomed out our benedictory prayers spontaneously with polished ease when I would call upon him to close our service when he graced us with his presence.

I was surprised when I heard he had been indicted on charges of embezzlement, but I was not too surprised.

But Ann Williams—Ann Williams was always full of surprises.

Chapter Eight

"The Sins of the Fathers, and a Little Cedar Tree"

One of the friends I had made in Tonkawa was the local librarian, Sally Caughlin. Sally was fascinating in a number of ways. Her precise speech alerted me to the fact that she was possessed of an enviable education. She welcomed all Tonkawans into her domain at the library, and she was always available to suggest a book on a number of topics or interests.

Sally had formerly been a nun, and when I met her, she was the mother of a growing family. She worked faithfully with the youth of the local Catholic church, pastored just as faithfully by Father Martin Reid.

Martin was the president of Tonkawa's ministerial alliance. When we had our meetings at the rectory, Father Martin always served homemade cookies with our coffee. When I met him, Martin was in his early sixties. Beyond the priestly collar, he was noticeable whenever he spoke because of his Irish accent. One of my regrets in life is not spending more time with this gracious soul. In the pride of youthfulness, I believe I must have thought I had little to learn, especially from someone so much my senior. Alas!

My first May in Tonkawa, I was invited to address the Tonkawa High School graduating class at the Baccalaureate service. It was held on a Sunday evening in the high school auditorium. My message warned the graduates of the danger of underestimating the enemy of our faith, Satan. Father Martin made an effort to speak to me as we left the auditorium. He spoke with a nod of the head, and he said to me only these memorable and encouraging words in his Irish cadence: "The man is humble." He spoke, and then he walked on. I still am touched and grateful to him for that moment, and I have always remembered him fondly.

Sally Caughlin needed someone to work on a project funded by The National Endowment for the Humanities. A history professor at Northern Oklahoma College, Dr. Bill Corbett, had written a brief history of the early days of Tonkawa in preparation for the celebration of the 90th anniversary of the founding of the city. Sally asked me to take his paper and to prepare from it a script for a slide-tape presentation for the celebration. I tape-recorded the script to accompany the slides. Sally had provided me with hundreds of photographs, many of them close to one hundred years old. The library would host the media presentation I prepared, and it would be kept on file for future use.

A further National Endowment for the Humanities project was on the topic of hazardous wastes. I headed up that project and led in community-wide discussions.

For some reason, a television station from Enid had nothing better to cover that evening than my presentation on hazardous wastes and deep injection wells. After my lecture and my leading of a discussion on the topic, the reporter thrust his microphone under my nose and the camera rolled. He asked; I answered. When I was able to see myself on television later that evening, my 15 minutes of fame was cut to a scant 15 seconds, *and I was misquoted.* In the short clip featuring my words, some careful and unscrupulous editing made me say something I very definitively did not say. No matter! I can't remember what I said, and neither could anyone else.

Years before, I logged three summers of construction work while in college. One of the friends I had developed on the work crew was an African American man named Charlie Harris. We ate lunch together every day, and I gravitated toward the areas where he was working whenever I could. He was about fifteen years older than I was, and he and his wife had two sons. For two decades I would visit him and his family when I returned to Mississippi, and both of my sons were privileged to meet him in the auto repair and body shop he ran in West Jackson.

During one of our lunches Charlie proclaimed and prophesied that one day he would turn on the television and see me on it. If he happened to be in a fifty-mile radius of Enid, Oklahoma, in 1983, he and a few others could have seen me on television.

Another Christmas was coming, and I needed a Christmas tree. I priced them at the local Food World grocery store. They were $7. I could not afford that, but Sally assured me that there were any number of cedar trees along their fence rows south of town, and I would be welcome to take one. Wes and I went for the drive after work one day, and we examined a mile or so of fence rows along the road. Cedar trees, yes, but too many were grown into the fence and were misshapen or had overwhelming brown patches. We came to the end of their property, and just a few feet beyond it, there was a perfect specimen near the fence. It was just on the other side so that it was not entangled in the fence. I knew it was not on their property, but I reasoned that cedar trees were a nuisance and that any farmer would be glad to get rid of it. All of that was in my mind as I delicately went through the barbed wire fence to trespass on the Caughlins' neighbor's property.

I began to saw with my hand saw. Who should arrive at that moment but the neighbor to the south! I met David for the first time. I had heard his name, and I knew that he was a deacon at First Baptist Church of Tonkawa. But I did not know then that he was enjoying the sight of a local pastor trespassing and stealing. I took the tree with me when I left, but I felt totally humiliated and embarrassed by the incident. And he, I later learned, was thoroughly delighted.

When we got back home that night, I wrote out a check for $7 and put with it a note of apology. I mailed it the next day. Two days later, on our front porch I found a large, paper grocery bag full of pecans. Buried but visible was my check for $7. David kindly had returned my check and restored a bit of my dignity.

Years later after our move from Iowa to Sedalia, Missouri, Christmas was once again approaching. My older son, Nathaniel, had become a young man. He had graduated from high school but still was living with us. One morning, I was in my office when a friend called to ask, "Eddie, is there anything I can do to help?"

"Help? What do you mean, Ron?"

"Oh, sheesh! You haven't heard, I guess. I just heard on the radio in the crime report that Nathaniel and Evan had been arrested for stealing a Christmas tree."

"WHAT!"

I ran down the hall, peeled out of the parking lot, sped down the hill to my driveway, and slammed on the brakes at home. I marched up the sidewalk to the front door, and snorting like a bull, I yelled at the top of the stairs: "Nathaniel, get out here!" Down the hall from his room came a sleepish and sheepish Nathaniel. He sat down for my diatribe. He explained that his good friend, Evan, had called him because Evan's wife, Bianca, wanted to go and find a Christmas tree. For some reason, instead of going to Evan's parents' farm, they went in Nathaniel's pickup down the local "lover's lane." Six-foot, seven-inch Evan stepped easily over the barbed wire fence and began sawing, just as I had some 20 years before. Well, not exactly as I had. It is more likely that I had crawled *under* the barbed wire fence.

At eleven o'clock at night, suddenly, headlights shone on them! Evan took the tree, threw it over the fence and into the back of the pickup, quick-stepped over the fence, and away they flew! Down country roads Nathaniel's testimony was like that of the poet, Francis Thompson: "I fled Him, down the nights and down the days; I fled Him, down the arches of the years; I fled Him, down the labyrinthine ways"[29] of the country roads in rural Pettis County. Finally, as he neared the Sedalia city limits, he saw flashing lights ahead and came to a stop by the side of the road. The Deputy Sheriff knew Nathaniel from Nathaniel's Police Cadet days. Nathaniel followed the deputy to the Sheriff's department. Nathaniel and Evan had to pay a $300 fine and do community service— picking up trash back at the scene of the crime on Cherry Tree Lane!

But the story doesn't end there. A year passed, and the time for the search for free Christmas trees was drawing close. One Wednesday evening in 2003, Nathaniel, Evan, and Bianca were attending the opening night of one of the Star Wars movies. I knew they had gone together to the movie, so I knew Evan and Bianca would be away from their home. My chainsaw and I had spent a few minutes earlier that day cutting down a dozen small cedar trees. I loaded them into the back of my pickup and drove to Evan's house. Under the cover of darkness, I crept up to their front door in the community of Clifton City, about seven miles east of my farm. I put a few trees on their front porch, and the rest I leaned against trees or bushes or fence posts. Their lawn was decorated with little Christmas trees.

---

[29] This verbiage is from Francis Thompson's poem, "The Hound of Heaven," Bartleby.com, November 2000, Accessed October 1, 2022, https://www.bartleby.com/236/239.html.

Nathaniel told me one year later that the day following my prank Evan accused, first his brother, and then, even his own father, of having placed the trees in the yard. With my sterling reputation and humble demeanor, no one could imagine that such a devious prank could be hatched in my innocent and angelic mind.

And yet, the story still is not over. A year following my prank, again at Christmas time, my family was gathered around the home computer for a Skype call with my missionary-nephew in India. I had emailed him and instructed him at some point of our visit to ask Nathaniel if Evan had ever figured out who put the Christmas trees in his yard. Nathaniel simply responded, "No, he never did." Nathaniel was nonplussed about how Matt could have known anything about the cedar tree prank. At that time I confessed. Nathaniel relayed the confession to Evan, and Evan said words and called me names, as far as I know, I have never been called before or since!

When I first upbraided Nathaniel over his misdeed, he was ashamed and humiliated by the incident, just as I, today, am ashamed of my overreaction at that time. How easy it is to see the fault in someone else's actions or words or thoughts, and how difficult it is to remember our own failings and failures—and thefts of cedar trees.

The Sunday after Nathaniel's name had appeared in the crime report, Lee Wagenknecht, one of the elders of our church, greeted Nathaniel. Lee sported his engaging smile and was laughing about the incident. That began to give me some perspective on the whole matter—that and the printed crime report from the local newspaper, *The Sedalia Democrat*. The radio crime report spoke of the theft of "a Christmas tree." That could have suggested to the hearer that a $35 tree from Lowe's had been stolen. The printed crime report in the local newspaper spelled out the fact that it had been "a little cedar tree."

Chapter Nine

"He Hates Pastors"

I was in my office one afternoon when one of my parishioners arrived for counseling. Her situation was that she urgently felt she needed to speak with her father about his spiritual condition before the Lord. I offered to visit with him myself, but when she felt that was not a good idea, I helped her plan her conversation with her father. Thankfully, he responded well to her overtures, and he asked Jesus to save him from his sin and to give him eternal life.

Over the years I have been privileged to minister to many of the parents of my parishioners, so that day in my office I asked her if she would like for me to visit him and . . . "No, Pastor Eddie! You don't understand. He HATES pastors!"

I had never met her father, but I had heard that he was a large man. The proverbial "mountain of a man."

As she said that, I was transported back to my junior high years. My best friend, Mike Webb, and I were just across the street from the home of Mary Ann Mobley. She was Miss America when I was in the second grade. Before Brandon was known as "The Boyhood Home of Eddie Brown," Mary Ann put Brandon, Mississippi, on the map. By the time I was twelve, she and her Hollywood husband were far away making movies with the likes of Elvis Presley.[30]

That Saturday afternoon, Mike and I were across the street from Mary Ann's house playing football with a few friends, most notably Ronnie Storey, John Storey, and, I think, Travis Tigrett, unless he was too sensible. (If Travis has no recollection of this, I quite understand. We tend to block out of our minds such traumatic events as this that took place near his home that afternoon. And, also, he may have been too young to remember it as clearly as I do. And also, he may not have been there!) Across the scrimmage line from us was Edmund—"Edmund the Terrible." Edmund was a few years older than we were, and with my being five foot six and 115 pounds, I thought he was the size of most professional wrestlers and NFL linemen—put together!

Ronnie got the ball from the quarterback and made a run at the line. I was in the backfield and had a perfect view of everything, even though I was backing up as the

---

[30] I recently viewed a YouTube video of Glen Campbell and Leon Russell. Leon Russell confessed that Elvis had brought him backstage once at a concert. He lamented that he had asked Elvis why he had consented to be in such awful movies. One of his awful movies included Mary Ann Mobley! Mary Ann had once babysat my friend Mike Webb.

play unfolded. Suddenly, Ronnie's forward progress was halted. "Edmund the Terrible" lifted him up off of the ground and momentarily held him chest-high and sideways—almost long enough for Ronnie to put his affairs in order—and with a ferocious growl he slammed him to the ground with a tremendous thud. It was just at that moment that I thought I heard my mother calling me for supper. I distinctly remember those dulcet tones when she would bellow for the third or fourth time for me to come to supper, and it was likely audible half a mile away as I was that day. At the same moment, I think Mike heard a similar summons, as too-tough-to-cry Ronnie lay moaning in a dazed and confused heap on the ground.

I had been a pastor in Tonkawa for just a short time when Grace Howard Tranbarger said she wanted to come and spend a Sunday afternoon with me and Wes. Grace was the teacher of the ladies' Sunday School class. I was too naïve to believe that I had done something to offend her, so my sole and selfish focus was wondering how I would prepare for the Sunday evening service if I had a Sunday afternoon guest for the entire afternoon.

The following Sunday arrived, and after the morning service, Grace followed us across the alley to the parsonage. Grace was a tall, slender woman of retirement age. Her brackish-colored hair was slightly thin and pretty tightly curled. She dressed in a utilitarian fashion with plain glasses and slacks made for comfort rather than for fashion. She had a very direct sort of manner, and she was highly intelligent. Her reputation as a Bible teacher was impressive, and the ladies in her class were devoted to her, Gladys Shelhamer among them. I had visited with Gladys and found in her a theological mind. She had read the entire eight-volume Systematic Theology of the founder of my esteemed seminary. I had read only two or three of the volumes! So if Gladys was impressed with Grace, I was sure that I would be also.

Wes set before us a simple meal, and then Grace joined us in our living room. My Sunday schedule was fairly rigid, even after a few months of pastoring. We ate; we napped; I studied and prepared for the evening service; I conducted the evening service; I came home; I ate a late dinner of fried eggs and bacon and toast; and I began my crash. When I arrived through the back door each Sunday evening, Wes would greet me with the words, "Happy Holiday." I quit my job every Sunday night and started again on Tuesday morning. Monday was my regular day off, in other words, and I tried not to think about church for those few hours. (Pastors understand.)

With Grace joining us that day, we ate; Wes, pregnant with our first child, fell asleep as we talked; and Grace began to get to know us. During that hours-long conversation, we were permitted a glimpse into her more personal life. After some forty years, I admit to being fuzzy on some of the details, but I believe she had worked in a clerical position for Conoco until her retirement, and her husband, Kirby, had worked in a maintenance position at Conoco until his retirement.

She then began to hint that she was enduring a somewhat unhappy marriage to a man who must have been a terrible ogre. He was difficult to please. No, he must have been impossible to please! He fairly demanded that his breakfast be prepared and on the table at 5:00

AM, his lunch by 11:00 AM, and his dinner at 4:00 PM. He kept beside him at all times a vicious animal that some supposed to be a dog, and perhaps it was a dog of some mongrel variety. It frequently growled at Grace and had threatened to bite her.

Grace would come alone to church, so we had never met or seen this husband of hers, but I began to form a mental picture of Kirby. The man was huge, by everything I had been led to believe. He was a cross between the giant farmer who hated pastors and Edmund the Terrible! When he spoke, it must have been with indecipherable growls and grunts, and when he breathed it may have been that he even emitted smoke like the dragon Smaug of *Hobbit* lore. The scowling face apparently was capable of only one other expression— that of menace. I was sure he carried about a rough club with the sharp end of a nail protruding from the larger end. There was no other reasonable conclusion. Grace was married to Hagar the Horrible!

Within a week or two of Grace's visit, I prepared my pastoral visit by calling ahead to their home. Kirby's four-acre compound on the southeastern side of Ponca City was fenced and bordered in front by a moat, a ditch some ten feet wide and nearly as deep. That seemed entirely appropriate. To gain entrance one had to cross a bridge and then open the double gates of woven wire. Since I had called ahead, the gate had been opened. Was this a trap of some sort? I was on hyper-alert.

I drove my little red station wagon in, and with some trepidation and a measure of tachycardia, I warily began my egress from my car. I sensed movement to my right and towards the back of the property. A man was exiting a metal building, and he was wiping his hands with a shop towel. The ogre was emerging from his lair.

I thought it best to show no fear, so I approached him and extended my hand. Finally, he stood before me. He looked up into my eyes, as he wiped his hands further. A gentle smile spread beneath the white mustache that brushed his top lip, and then it continued across his face. Had he removed his cap, I could have seen his white hair, neatly parted on one side. He reached out a clean hand, and said, "Why don't you come inside, Pastor? I can probably scare up some coffee." I walked behind him and noticed he was slightly stooped, but even if he could straighten up, still I was a couple of inches taller than he was. Since he was about 140 pounds, I outweighed him by nearly 20 pounds, and he was even an inch or two shorter than Grace. I wondered how this could be the man she had described.

Kirby sat down first and leaned back in his easy chair with one leg up in the chair with his foot under the knee of his other leg. His easy smile was relaxed, and he indicated a chair for me across the room from his throne, and then I saw the beast which lay at his feet. Indeed, it did growl. Every time that I shifted in my chair, his dog growled. If I crossed or uncrossed my legs, it lifted its head and growled.

As I think about it today, I am reminded of one other man and his dog. We were living in Eagle Grove, Iowa, at the time. It was a small town like Tonkawa, and, from the Chamber of Commerce, I was able to get a list of people who had recently moved into town. I would frequently go to invite to church the newcomers to our town. On one Saturday morning I was out doing some visiting. I met a man and his wife who had moved to Eagle Grove from Montana or some western state.

I was uncomfortable right from the start. Perhaps what made me nervous was his constant reference to guns and fights he had been in when people crossed him or said the wrong thing, or maybe it was that he kept his twitchy German shepherd between me and the door. Or maybe it was that every time my heart beat the dog growled. Yeah, I think that was part of it.

I asked what he did for a living, and he showed me a very amateurish photo album. It came out that he had never been able to keep a job. Someone was "always against" him.

So now he was a freelance photographer. That way he didn't have a boss. "Nobody tells me what to do!" he insisted.

His plan was to go to the mayor and ask if he could put together a pictorial city brochure for the city of Eagle Grove. "Sounds like a good plan to me. I'll leave so you can get started on it."

"Whaddya' think of my pictures?"

What would you say if he and his dog asked you what you thought of his pictures? I gushed shamelessly.

As I began to think about my exit, he told me about the fight he and his brother-in-law had recently had . . . "right out there," he said as he pointed to the spot in the backyard beneath the tree. Once again, I thought I heard my mother calling me. Yes, I was sure of it. I thanked him for his time and said goodbye.

The afternoon I had stopped by to visit Grace and Kirby, Grace was running errands. I remember nothing of my conversation with Kirby except that there was nothing that was negative or threatening or anything but positive and gentlemanly.

I was beginning to learn that I needed to form my own opinions of people, and I needed to avoid taking someone else's word for another's character.[31] I, too, am capable of misreading others and, in turn, misleading others about them.

A month or so later Grace invited Wes and me to go with her to a Family Camp sponsored by a mission group in eastern Oklahoma. The campgrounds were near Tahlequah. Wes and I drove to Ponca City to pick Grace up, and she mentioned stopping by the Will Rogers Museum at Claremore while we were en route.

I admit that I was leery of going to this camp. Once again, it interfered with my sermon preparation time, but to be honest, I had never heard of any of the speakers. I wondered what they could possibly teach me. After all, I had gone to Dallas Theological Seminary!

One of the great leaders of pastors in the last century was a man who had repented of a very public moral failure and had become, once again, useful to the Lord. Like Dr. Richard Seume said of Samson, "The Hair Can

---

[31] Proverbs 18:17 says, "The one who states his case first seems right, until the other comes and examines him" (English Standard Version). In counseling couples over the years I saw many times that the first one who presented his or her case for what was ailing in the marriage very generally *seemed* to offer an accurate assessment until the other presented her or his side of the issue.

Grow Again."[32] Gordon MacDonald had written winsome books on marriage and on child-rearing, and then he entered a season of life in which his heart was turned from the Lord. By the grace of God, his wife forgave him, and every time I heard him speak after his failure, and in many of his publications, he alluded to his failure, his wife's forgiveness, and the Lord's gracious forgiveness and restoration. Before his failure was public, he was speaking at a pastors' conference at Dallas Theological Seminary. He began his address to the two thousand pastors by referring to a time when he had been in seminary in Denver. His words were met with uproarious laughter from the Dallas men and women in attendance when he said: "Just so you know, there *IS* another seminary!"

It has often been said, "You can always tell a Dallas Man. You just can't tell him *much*." I suppose I was still in that Dallas Man mindset when I was going to the Family Camp of "Go-Ye Mission." In that summer of 1980, I would have been almost thirty years of age. I had conducted my first wedding and my first funeral. I had preached some fifty sermons, taught another fifty Bible classes, and had spoken at one youth retreat. I had recovered from the profound humility that I had felt the first week of my seminary experience.

---

[32] Richard H. Seume, *Shoes for the Road*, (Chicago: Moody Press, 1974), 77ff. Dr. Seume was the chaplain at Dallas Seminary while I was there. He was a retired pastor and was revered by the students and faculty! As a kidney patient on dialysis, he gave his last years to the seminary and its students. He refers to Judges 16:22.

Upon our graduation and our departure from our beloved seminary with our degrees which were called "Master of Theology," Dr. Howard Hendricks had warned us not to kid ourselves. We would never be masters of theology! And yet, there is always the subtle temptation to believe in our own significance, and if we doubt that, then we must ask ourselves how we feel when we sense that we have been slighted or not treated as the important persons that we believe ourselves to be. If we are aware that we have been so treated or slighted, then we are guilty of pride. There is nothing quite so ugly as a sight of our own pride.

We arrived at the camp and checked into our cabins. The sessions that I remember were taught by a minister at the mission, Kurt Marquardt, and a pastor in from the Cleveland area—from Elyria, Ohio: Don Engram. Pastor Engram spoke on the wonderful book of Second Timothy, and Rev. Marquardt on the Sermon on the Mount. Again I discovered that there were other seminaries. How wonderful is the Lord to be able, by His mighty power, to use a vast variety of His people, each with stunningly different gifts and talents, with advanced education and with the learning that comes only from spending time with the Master. He can use anyone who is humbly submitted to Him![33]

---

[33] The religious leaders were forced back on their heels when they saw the boldness of the disciples of Jesus after His resurrection. They were preaching in the Name of Jesus, and they spoke confidently of Him as the only source of salvation from sin. Yet they marveled that none of the disciples had been trained in the rabbinical schools. All that was truly necessary for usefulness to the Lord was summed up in the lovely phrase that described the disciples: "they had been with Jesus" (AV). In

When Grace was in her mid-seventies, she developed shingles. She checked herself into a nursing home for the duration so that she could receive the care she needed. When that malady passed and before the year was out, she was soon to experience yet one more. I visited her in that same nursing home where she told me she had been diagnosed with pancreatic cancer. It is a painful and soul-sucking type of cancer, and, those who endure it do so for about six months from first diagnosis. Grace entrusted herself to the One who could deliver from death unto a heavenly country, "a city . . . whose builder and maker is God."[34]

Four years had passed in our time in Tonkawa, but it was before Grace had been diagnosed with the cancer which would take her. We needed someone to take care of our dog for a week while we were away. Kirby said, "Bring Eustace over! We'll have a good time." On our way home from that trip we passed by the east side of Ponca City and their home. It was going to be after Kirby's bedtime, so we arranged for him to leave Eustace loose inside his fence. I pulled the car up on the bridge and shone the headlights on the gate. I opened the gate so that Eustace could come to get into our car. Eustace hesitated. He actually looked back toward their house,

---

Acts 4:13 Luke wrote, "Now as they observed the confidence of Peter and John and understood that they were uneducated and untrained men, they were amazed, and *began* to recognize them as having been with Jesus" (NASB).

[34] The author of Hebrews wrote of Abraham and his faith that he was looking "for a city whose builder and maker is God" (Heb. 11:10 AV).

and then, with some coaxing, he followed me to the back of our car. He liked Kirby as much as I did.

Chapter Ten

"Just Up the Road"

One Sunday a couple visited our little church. We were still so small that every visitor was conspicuous, and every visitor felt conspicuous. This family was from a small community a bit north and east of Tonkawa. Howard and Gaylene had three children, and the children were being parented by two adults who had not had the benefit of being parented by a mother and a father who cared for them. Howard and Gaylene understood the biological process that delivered their children, but they had no idea how to love them and nurture them and to help them feel secure and significant and loved. How could they? They had never felt those things themselves.

When I went by the next week to visit with the family, I was warmly welcomed into their home. I will tell you, it was not the reception that a pastor would always receive on such a visit. At times, there was an element of suspicion. After all, on that list of most-trusted and distrusted professions, pastors have now made their way downward to that unenviable position on the list between attorneys and used-car salesmen.

I love what Samuel Johnson said of someone he did not know well. His biographer, James Boswell, wrote: "Johnson observed, that 'he did not care to speak ill of any man behind his back, but he believed the gentleman was an *attorney*.'"[35] Disparaging words are frequently spoken of individuals in my own profession, and, truth be known, I have spoken some of them. Pastors do not always deserve respect, and I am sad to say that, likewise, I have not always deserved respect.

Nonetheless, Howard and Gaylene held me high in admiration, and for that I felt very sorry for them. It was not that I had done anything deserving of their disrespect, but for them I was a significant person, and they felt honored by my presence in their home. In my own eyes I was certainly nothing special.

Howard's work was the early shift from 7:00 to 3:00, and he was always anxious to get out of his factory-worker uniform, take a shower to wash away the grit of the day, and then get on with his hobby. His only hobby, I came to understand, was to shop the clearance sections of the big stores like Walmart, Target, and, in those days, K-Mart. After he cleaned up, he would rush out the door of his home on the days the new items regularly went on clearance. Those three stores were in Ponca City, about

---

[35] James Boswell, *The Life of Samuel Johnson*, LL.D. Vol. 1: 1709–1775 (London: J.M. Dent & Co., 1906), 393. First published 1791.

fifteen minutes away from their home. He would fill his small car with his treasures and then take them to a section of his basement where he kept an astounding assortment of Christmas wrapping paper. After he got to know me and trust me, he took me to the basement to show me the incredible number of wrapped presents he had.

“Howard, what will you do with all of this?”

He told me something of his life story. His earliest memories were of lying on the floor with his blanket. He was beside the bed where his mother earned her living. He had no memories of his father, and his mother used the little money she brought in to pay for beer and cigarettes. With government help there was food, if his mother couldn’t figure out a way to sell the food stamps for cash so she could buy the things which gave her some brief escape from the downward swirl in the toilet bowl that was her life.

The presents he wrapped would go to children who had no parents to buy gifts for them. Since Howard had a decent income, he enjoyed immensely the opportunity to buy Christmas gifts for children who endured a situation similar to the one he endured as a child.

As I got to know Howard and Gaylene, I saw in their eyes that desperate longing for the approval of someone they viewed as a surrogate parent. They were just a few years older than I, but their eagerness to do or say anything I might look on approvingly was as palpable as it was pathetic. Only one other time had I seen such hunger for approval in someone’s face.

After I graduated from high school, I went to a Youth for Christ summer camp with forty high school students from Jackson, Mississippi, and the surrounding area. We had gotten off the bus in Toccoa Falls, Georgia, and I was exploring the campgrounds where we would spend the week. Steve was six foot two and still wearing braces. I had not noticed him on the bus, but he apparently had noticed me. He walked up to me with a grin that showed the rubber bands on his braces. He had brown, curly hair and was well-built—built like an athlete. As he walked up to me, he reached out with his right hand and pulled the hair in my sideburns. Instinctively, I grabbed his wrist with my left hand, and with my right hand I bent his fingers back as far as I could. He dropped to his knees instantly. I had never seen him before that moment. Talk about an impression!

The few short weeks of summer passed too quickly, and I found myself checking into my college dormitory. There was a suite of four rooms which shared a bathroom. In one of the front two rooms were two boys from Louisiana, and in the other a boy from Brandon's list of arch-rivals. At the top of that list was Pearl High School, and that guy was from Pearl. His roommate, Mac, was from Vicksburg.

Mac had been offered a swimming scholarship to LSU, but when he had gone to the campus, he asked at the campus information center for directions to the natatorium. The young woman at the desk could not tell him how to get there. He decided then and there to go to a smaller college. I believe he is now a medical doctor in Vicksburg.

Across the hall from my room were two mismatched young men: Tom, who proclaimed himself an atheist, and the other was the son of a leader in the Southern Baptist Church of Mississippi. Ralph was preaching at everyone to forsake their habits that were leading them to hell!

That "preacher" had discovered that I was a Christian, and in one of our group encounters when he was preaching against the evils of smoking, he said, "Eddie, show them what's in your pocket." I carried a small New Testament that an older Christian from Brandon High School had given to me. I pulled it out. "Great!" I thought. "Now all these guys will associate me with Ralph's brand of legalistic Christianity."

This conversation took place in the dorm room of Mac and Billy. Of all the places on the planet, Billy was from Pearl, Mississippi. Brandon and Pearl, in those days, did not get along. The rivalry was too intense. Billy's room became the hangout for several commuters from Pearl, and that brought Bobby into my life. My first night in the dorm, Bobby was sleeping over on the floor of Billy's room. He walked into my room with his cigarette dangling from his lower lip. It looked as though it had been glued there. In one hand he was holding a pipe wrench and spanking his other hand with it. Oh, and he was in his white underwear. Yes, just his underwear. With cowboy boots!

I was minding my own business in my dorm room getting things organized for the momentous event of the first day of college classes. Bobby made quite an impression and confirmed everything I had thought about the hoods from Pearl, but Billy turned out to be an extraordinarily nice guy.

Across the hall from Mac and Billy were the two from Louisiana. One with the most nondescript and fictitious-sounding names imaginable was intelligent and serious, even cultured. His roommate, however, only spoke hick in the colorful and country and Cajun expressions that would have made Larry the Cable Guy proud.

I was reveling in what had developed. There were four rooms with seven people, and I was alone in my dorm room. I did not have a roommate. Within a couple of days some of the guys from Pearl discovered that fact. One of their friends was looking for a dormitory room. Within the week I had a new roommate. From Pearl! His name was Larry. He got the top bunk.

I had to admit after the first few weeks, that even Bobby, the underwear model, was a nice enough guy. Billy would become a good friend, and when Larry got married a few months later, I would be a groomsman. A groomsman for someone from Pearl!

Larry proved to be the most interesting of the young men from Pearl. He continued to commute and rarely stayed on campus. One of his high school jobs had been running moonshine. He drove a red hot rod. It was a 1962 Chevy Impala with a souped-up engine that had some 400 horsepower. It had the coveted four-on-the-floor, and he let me drive it. Under the back seat it had a tank for moonshine. Why would a car have such a tank? Larry and I were both from a dry county in Mississippi. It was illegal to sell alcohol in Rankin County, but moonshine was produced in stills like the ones that were on *The Andy Griffith Show*. Someone had to deliver the contraband, so Larry was a moonshine runner during his high school days. He was "Larry the Moonshine Runner" since there was no such thing then as "Larry the Cable Guy."

Larry was rarely there with us in the dorm, and that meant that his bed was available.

It was not long before I ran into Steve on campus—Steve who had pulled my sideburns! He was insecure and needy, and he played the guilt card since I was "rich," and he wasn't. I, of course, was anything but rich. I had grown up in a loving and stable home with both parents who sought to be the best parents they were able to be. My father's income was a typical blue-collar income, and it paid the bills but bought nothing extravagant and nothing extra. From the seventh grade on, I had been buying my own clothes and paying for anything additional that I might want. I had worked hard in high school, and I had saved enough for my first year of college. Steve made himself out to be poor, and, I am sure that he was.

Steve wanted to occupy the empty bed in my dorm room since my roommate was rarely there. I did feel sorry for him. I said he could, but he was perpetually whining about his lot in life.

During this period, Steve wanted to repay my kindness by having me over to meet his mother and his sister. We went one evening to their home for dinner. I was just a freshman in college, but at the dinner table were three individuals who desperately wanted my approval. All were solicitous of my thoughts about my meal of roast beef. "How was it? Did you like it?" All three were wide-eyed and anxious for any words of approval that I—just a boy from Brandon—might offer.

At another time, back in the dorm room, Steve was actually becoming belligerent enough to provoke a shoving match. I told him he couldn't stay there any longer.

That same depth of insecurity and approval-seeking was what I saw in Howard and Gaylene some years later. In spite of their poor self-images, both had a positive love for others, especially for those who struggled with substance abuse or with alcohol.

Howard called me on a Saturday morning to see if I would go with him to visit a friend of his who was on a heart transplant list. Howard wanted to share with Vinny the Jesus who had saved him from his sin. Specifically, he wanted me to tell Vinny about Jesus.

Howard drove to my house to pick me up. We would go to Vinny's apartment together. Vinny owned an "adult entertainment" establishment. There, he had met Vicky, the woman who would become his wife. She had worked there as a dancer. On the way to visit his friend, Howard explained to me that Vinny had suffered ten heart attacks. He was on the heart transplant list. Most of all, though, Vinny needed the Lord in his life.

His apartment was somewhere outside of Ponca City. Vicky was not at home, so Howard introduced me to Vinny, and we began to talk and to get to know one another. He was not yet forty years old, and his heart was so weak that he could walk only a couple of hundred feet before he had to sit and recover. The damage to his heart from the many heart attacks was tremendous. His heart was barely functioning. He had no assurance that he would live long enough to get the heart transplant.

I asked Vinny if anyone had ever shown him from the Bible how he could know that he knew Jesus as Lord and Savior. He said that no one had. I asked if he would mind if I did. He was eager to hear about Jesus.

I took him to the Scriptures—to Romans 3:23, which says, "For all have sinned and fall short of the glory of God."[36] I read to him the verse, and he followed along in my Bible as I did so. I then asked him what the word "all" meant. Like so many others that I've asked that question, he shook his head and moved his hands up and away from each other and proclaimed: "Everybody!"

"Even me?" I asked.

"Yes!"

"Does that mean, Vinny, that you have sinned?"

"Yes." The Lord was working in his heart and had convicted him of sin.[37]

I explained that everyone had fallen short of the glory of God in the sense that "no one is as-good-as-God-is-good." The Lord is perfectly righteous. He has no sin. He is holy and separate from sin in His nature. We considered that with God's being perfect and our being imperfect—His righteousness demands that no sin be in His presence. What can be done about our sin?

---

[36] Rom. 3:23 (AV).

[37] Theologians speak of the *ordo salutis*—the order of salvation. By that term they mean to suggest the order of the acts of God in working our salvation from sin. Conviction of sin by the Holy Spirit (John 16:8–11) is one of the logically discrete elements in the seamless application of our redemption by the Lord. John Murray is a major influence on my thinking in this matter. See John Murray, *Redemption Accomplished and Applied*, (Grand Rapids: Eerdmans, 1955), 79–87, and Wayne Grudem, *Systematic Theology: An Introduction to Biblical Doctrine*, Second Edition (Grand Rapids: Zondervan Academic, 2020), 816–17.

We turned then to Romans 6:23, and again I read it to him: "For the wages of sin is death, . . ." We talked about wages being something that we earn and deserve, so the verse was saying that what we earned and what we deserved by our sin was death! It speaks of death as a penalty for sin, but there is in the Scripture the implication that death speaks also of separation from God forever—for all eternity. Again, what could be done about our sin? What could we do? Absolutely nothing! We needed someone to save us from the penalty of our sin.

I then read the rest of the verse: ". . . but the gift of God is eternal life in Christ Jesus our Lord." There it is! A gift from God! Here is the contrast between earning and deserving something—death—and the possibility of receiving something we did not earn or deserve—a gift. We deserved death. God offered a gift—life—eternal life in the presence of the God who loves us.

What the Bible reveals is that Jesus died in our place, and He died for our sins.

We turned next to Romans 5:8 and read: "But God demonstrates His own love for us in that, while we were yet sinners, Christ died for us." Vinny and I talked about the fact that Jesus died for us "while we were still sinners." He didn't wait for us to try to clean up our lives. He died for us while we were sinners, because of His great love for us. No one else has ever loved us so.

That had been the answer that Howard and Gaylene had discovered some years before. Howard and Vinny had been friends from youth, and Vinny had seen the changes that Jesus had brought to Howard's life. It was that difference that made him willing to listen to us that day—

that difference as well as the very real and sincere love and concern which Howard had for Vinny.

Next, I opened my Bible to the Gospel of John, chapter one. In verses eleven and twelve we read together these words about Jesus: "He came to His own, and those who were His own did not receive Him. But as many as received Him, to them He gave the right to become children of God, *even* to those who believe in His name, . . ."[38]

I explained that the Bible was saying that Jesus had come to His own people, the Jewish people, and that they had rejected Him. But not everyone did! Not everyone rejected Jesus! Some received Him as Messiah and as Lord and as Savior. How had they done that? They had believed in Him. They had trusted in Him. They had come to rely on Him and on His death to pay the penalty for their sin.

That is what I had done as an eleven-year-old. That was what Howard had done as a man in his thirties. I then asked Vinny if he wanted to call on Jesus to save him from his sins. He understood that day that he had to repent of his sins. We explained repentance as "a change of mind that leads to a change of life." With repentance there is a change of mind about God and a coming to understand that He is perfectly righteous and just but that He still loves us. Repentance also involves a change of mind about sin—our own sin—and a coming to understand how utterly offensive it is before a holy and righteous God. He finds sin repulsive, and we are led by

---

[38] John 1:11–12 (NASB).

His Spirit to come to the point that we want to turn from sin and turn to the Savior. We do that by simple faith in Jesus.

At one place in the New Testament a man from Philippi asked Silas and Paul how he could be saved. Paul replied: "Believe on the Lord Jesus Christ, and you will be saved, . . ."[39] The New Testament teaching is clear that salvation is by grace and through faith.[40]

That day Vinny called on the Lord Jesus to forgive his sins and to give him eternal life. Jesus said, "In the same way, I tell you, there is joy in the presence of the angels of God over one sinner who repents."[41]

Vinny began to attend church regularly. He sold the "adult entertainment" establishment. About two months had passed when Howard called to say that Vinny had gotten the call from the university hospital that a heart had become available for his heart transplant. Sadly, though the transplant was technically successful, Vinny had developed an infection and died two weeks later.

At his funeral I was able to tell his story to his friends—the story of how Vinny had called out to Jesus to save him and that he had trusted in Jesus as Lord and Savior. Vinny is forever with the Lord.

One day Howard's father-in-law called me and invited me for coffee. I had met him when he had visited church

---

[39] Acts 16:31 (NASB).

[40] Eph. 2:8–10. My friend, John Neibergall, well defined faith when he wrote these words to me in private correspondence: "Genuine, redemptive faith is a God-initiated, Spirit breathed, biblically-informed, tethered, nurtured, and lived-out personal relationship and devotion to Jesus Christ."

[41] Luke 15:10 (NASB).

a few times. For some reason he felt that he should help me understand the provisions he had put in his will. While we sat in the coffee shop he had suggested, he told me of his concerns for the way that his daughter and his son-in-law handled their money. They had recently purchased a nicer house in another part of town, and it seemed like a wise investment to me. It certainly had a better resale value than their former one that was very much like mine. No, that wasn't his concern. He went on to speak of Howard's "shopping addiction" and expressed that he imagined Howard would go through any inheritance that he would leave the two of them. He then went on, crassly, to explain that Gaylene was his only daughter, and she was unsatisfactory to him because he had wanted a son.

Adjusted for inflation, the estate would have been somewhat over a million dollars today. He had decided to leave it in trust for his three grandchildren. They would be able to access the money when they had completed college and had entered into a career. By that time the amount of the trust would have been closer to $2,000,000. He wanted me to understand so that I could help his daughter, Gaylene, and his son-in-law to understand.[42]

Despite his insecurities and his compulsions, Howard was a man who loved the Lord who had saved

---

[42] A great many people have shared with me a great many things over the years. The conversations between a pastor and a parishioner are private conversations. Many of the persons of whom I speak in this book are no longer living or have given me permission to share their stories.

him, and he loved sharing with others in any way he could. He and Gaylene have joined Vinny in the Place that Jesus has prepared for them and for all those who love Him and follow Him. Howard lived for Jesus, and he more and more realized his value in the eyes of Jesus who had died for him.

In one of my seminary classes, Professor Phil Douglass quoted a mentor of his, Jack Miller, as saying: "Your sin is worse than you ever dared to admit, but you are loved more than you ever dared to hope."

Chapter Eleven

"Silver and Black '57"

I was out for my weekly prayer walk one October Saturday night, and that particular night I had gone east a few blocks and a mile or so south of Tonkawa on a country road. I must admit that I had been a bit discouraged. On those walks I would pray over my little church, and I would pray for passion and power to preach the Word of God the following morning. It was a clear night, and the stars and moon lit my way. After about forty-five minutes, I was walking through the back door and into the kitchen.

Wes was a bit mysterious. "You got a phone call while you were gone."

"Oh? Who?"

"It's a surprise."

I waited only fifteen minutes before the phone rang again. He wouldn't give me a clue other than the sound of a voice I had not heard in over ten years.

"Rod?" I asked.

Rod responded, "How are you doin', man?"

In my second year of college I was working for Youth For Christ in Jackson, Mississippi. There were half a dozen college guys who led Campus Life Clubs, as they were called then. My club was on the southwest side of Jackson in Forest Hill High School. We would have meetings in the home of a YFC supporter one night a week, and I would have 20–25 high school students join me each week as we met in the pool house in back of his home.

One night a sharp 1957 Chevy rumbled up and stopped on the street where we were meeting. A nice-looking high school junior hopped out and came up to our group. He had recently moved to Forest Hill from California, and his nickname was "Chick." That was how he referred to girls, and soon it was what he was called. His real name was Rod Kendrick.

Rod had long and wavy blondish-brown hair. He was someone the girls noticed. You've seen the sort of thing. A few girls are walking through the school hallways carrying their books in their arms, and after they pass by the new guy, all three giggle out loud.

That night Rod listened intently to what I was saying about how to become a Christian. At the end of my talk I asked if anyone wanted to ask Jesus to be his or her Lord and Savior. Rod raised his hand. His conversion was real, and Rod began to grow in his faith.

The following year I no longer worked for Youth For Christ, and Rod and I occasionally bumped into one another. A couple of years later I moved to Dallas for seminary, and then four years after that, on to Tonkawa, Oklahoma, as a pastor of my first church. Another few years passed, and Rod called on a Saturday night.

After I brought him up to speed on the intervening years of my life, I asked him to tell me about himself. He told me that he had not been walking with the Lord.

One night he was on his way to his girlfriend's house for dinner, and on his way, he fell asleep while driving. He ran off the road, went through a field, and hit a tree with his Camaro. Someone saw the wrecked car and called for an ambulance. A few days later, Rod stirred from one surgery and fully realized that the surgeon had removed one of his legs and was going to have to remove the other one. He lapsed into a coma. When he regained consciousness, he had lost both of his legs.

One of my greatest interpersonal and pastoral gifts is to be able to cry. (I am being facetious, which is something my readers might not realize since many of them— perhaps millions of them—don't know me.) My grandfather used to say that my grandmother would cry when he left and cry when he came home. After I married and had a family of my own, my father would stifle his tears whenever we would leave to travel back to our home some distance away. Every time my daughter and her family leave for their African home, I hug my beloved daughter tightly and stifle tears in the airport. The flood is unleashed when I get back to the car. My inability to keep from crying when someone is hurting must be genetic.

Some ten years later, Rod was being interviewed by a staff writer for the *Clarion-Ledger*. Photographs in the paper showed him doing his workout at a local gym. He had participated in several wheelchair races and triathlons. As he shared his story, he told of how he had called me on that Saturday night. Here is the account from the *Clarion-Ledger* in the "People" section one Sunday:

> Reality set in when Kendrick went to live with his parents in Terry in December 1982. "I became intensely depressed," he says. "I was withdrawn, frustrated . . . totally devastated." One day he phoned a friend, Eddie Brown, who was living in Oklahoma. "Eddie had led me to the Lord in 1971," Kendrick says. "I called him, told him what had happened, and he just started crying right there on the phone. It freaked me out that he had so much compassion. It humbled me, but it also gave me joy that somebody cared that much." Brown recommended Kendrick read *Joni*, a book by Joni Eareckson, an outstanding swimmer who had been paralyzed in a diving accident. "That book was a big turning point for me," he said. "She quoted several Scriptures in there, and when I read that book, it was as if God reached down and put his arms around me. It was as if he said, 'It's OK, you're still worth something to me. It's OK, you can still do things. It's OK, I can still use you.' "That was when my rehabilitation really began."[43]

A year passed, and I called Rod back one day as Thanksgiving neared in 1983. I told him that I wanted to

---

[43] J.D. Schwaim, "Stretching Life to the Limit," *The Clarion-Ledger*, July 7, 1991.

record his answer and share it with my church on the following Sunday. I then asked him this question: "Rod, what are you thankful for?" He didn't hesitate, and I could tell he was speaking through lips that were smiling.

I'm thankful that I'm still alive—that I can worship the Lord still—that I can praise Him and sing praises to Him—that I still have the use of my mind so that I can understand the Word of God and still bring praises to Him. I'm thankful just for everything in the world, and that's for the air we breathe, for the trees—just everything. More importantly, I'm thankful that Jesus Christ died on the cross for us— that we can have eternal salvation. And I think everyone should be thankful for that.

I then asked, "Rod, in 1 Thessalonians 5:18 it says: 'In everything give thanks, for this is the will of God in Christ Jesus concerning you.' How is it that you, without your legs, are able to have a thankful spirit? Did you just wake up thankful, or was it a process? Tell me about that."

I was still conscious in the emergency room when they took my right leg off above the knee. I was then in a coma for five weeks. When I came out of the coma, I realized they had taken my other leg off. All the time I was in the rehab center, they told me I was going to go through a state of depression, but I didn't do that. Well, when I got home, they said, that's when it will hit. And I was home about three months and started reading my Bible again because I had been putting the Lord out of my mind—just putting Him behind me. There's a certain Scripture in Corinthians—chapter 12, Second Corinthians, I think, where he [the Apostle Paul] went up to heaven and to keep him from being so boastful, the devil put a thorn under his flesh, and he just prayed and asked God to get rid of that thorn. And I prayed, three times—three separate nights that the Lord would just perform a miracle and give me some new legs. Well, after I prayed that third time, I got something far much greater than my legs. This was a total peace with my condition. I didn't care about my legs—I don't care about 'em now.

My thankfulness has grown because, since I've gotten that peace of mind, I've been able to grow spiritually beyond my imagination. I thought I'd never get to this point in my spiritual maturity. I thought it'd just take forever and ever. [But I grew] and I just constantly thank the Lord. It wasn't a quick process, but it was one worth—well-worth waiting for.

Rod Kendrick, training for a marathon

A decade passed, and Rod and I corresponded occasionally. One December we were home in Brandon, Mississippi, for Christmas. While we were there, I told my three children that I wanted them to meet a joyful Christian. I know many joyful Christians, but I don't know many as joyful as Rod Kendrick. We drove to the Stewart Lighting Company on South State Street in

Jackson, and when we entered the shop, I asked for directions to the area where Rod worked. I told them I did not want to be announced because I wanted to surprise him. We had not seen each other in nearly twenty years. During those years his hairline had receded, and mine had run for cover and had disappeared over the other side of the hill. My children at that time were aged 13, 11, and 5. As we approached the area where he worked, I saw a couple of cash registers on a low countertop that surrounded, on three sides, a man in a wheelchair. I walked up to the counter and placed my hands on the counter. I said nothing. I looked at the man in the wheelchair as he pushed the big wheels with his strong hands. The chair turned, and a smile spread across his face as he came to greet a customer.

"Can I help you?" he said.

Still I said nothing. I had something of a gentle smile on my face as I saw him once again after those two decades. The next words were words I've heard most of my life. Both of my names are so frequently said together—like Billy Bob in Arkansas. Rod exclaimed, "Eddie Brown!"

I introduced my children, Nathaniel, Anna, and Caleb, and we visited for a time until his phone was ringing. I said my goodbyes, and when we got to the car, Nathaniel was horrified at what I had said to Rod. "Dad! Did you hear what you said to him?"

"No. What did I say?" Nathaniel could not believe that I had said those words to my friend in his wheelchair.

I called Rod in a day or two to relay the story to him. I thought he would enjoy a laugh. Rod said, "What did you say to me? That you liked my shoes?"

I laughed at that, and then I told him what had upset Nathaniel so much: "Rod, it was so good to see you walking with the Lord!"[44]

------

[44] Rod Kendrick tells his full story in his book *My Thousand Pound Gorilla.*

Chapter Twelve

____

"Day Is Done"

The phone rang one morning, and this time it was
Wanda Gillispie calling to tell me her father, Roy
Cornwell, had been taken to the hospital in Ponca City.
That afternoon I drove the twenty miles to the hospital to
visit with Roy. It had been a year since Roy had helped
me put a cane bottom into a chair that had belonged to
my grandmother. We worked on it several afternoons in
his garage, and he guided me through the process and
allowed me to do the work. I placed the pre-woven cane
bottom over the channel that was chiseled into the
wooden chair bottom. Then I lightly hammered the spline
that pushed the woven cane into the channel. The spline
held it fast. I then trimmed the edges away from the
outside edge of the spline. Good as new!

Roy was in his eighties and had "coke-bottle" glasses.
He and Edith lived in a clapboard house on West Grand,

built in the early days of Tonkawa, some twenty years after the Sooners staked their claims. Their house had an attractive front porch and nice shade trees.

When I walked into the hospital room to see Roy, I found him sitting up in bed without his glasses. The bed was unusual. It was of the trapeze bar variety, and the aluminum bars from which the trapeze hung had the look of a framing structure for a large box. The metal trapeze bar hung over the bed so that the patient could pull himself up when sitting up in bed. Roy, without his glasses, was staring at the bars and trying to figure out where he was. He sensed movement as I came in and turned to look at me. I said, "Hi, Roy. I'm so sorry to see you here."

He replied, "Eddie, what am I doing inside this air conditioner?"

Roy was in the early stages of Alzheimer's, and I explained to him where he was and that this was just the frame for the trapeze structure of his bed. He chuckled because it finally made sense.

We visited for a time, and as I was walking out of the room he joked, "Hey, Eddie. Tell the nurses to come get me out of this air conditioner."

Ted and Lena Carpenter were two other regulars at Tonkawa Bible Church. Lena had tight curls in her gray hair and also had thick and heavy bifocal glasses. Ted loved to talk of cars he had owned and of his many occupations over the years. Lena was shy around strangers, but that was not the half of it. She suffered from a severe case of agoraphobia. She welcomed me into her home, but it was very difficult for her to leave her home and to come to church. And yet, with Ted by her side, she was willing to come. Still, like others with agoraphobia, she would sit near the door in case a severe panic seized her and thrust her out and away from the small group gathered at Tonkawa Bible Church on any Sunday morning.

Ted relished telling me about his job in 1929 in Colorado. The bridge over the Royal Gorge was being built, and he was among the many who went there for a job. It was the beginning of the Great Depression, so work was scarce. His first morning he walked up near the edge of the vast chasm and looked down a thousand feet to the Arkansas River far below. He turned on his heels and shakily walked away. He could not be there, and he couldn't begin to think of working there.

One Sunday after church, Ted told me that the doctor had discovered that he had an aneurysm in an artery around his stomach. The surgery was scheduled. Ted did not survive. Lena was suddenly alone. She was terribly and fearfully alone. Their children lived some distance away. A big, iridescent green Buick was in the tiny garage next to the house. Lena had not driven in years. She felt she would need to drive the half mile to the grocery store and to run errands. She asked if I would teach her how to drive again.

The mirrors on the sides of the car had just inches of clearance as I backed it out of the cramped garage that was made for a day when cars were smaller. Once out, I believed she intended to leave it out. With her poor vision she couldn't get it out alone.

North of Tonkawa near the cemetery was the old prisoner-of-war camp site with some paved roads that were rarely used. I drove Lena there and got out of the car. Lena did too. She hobbled around to the other side. She was growing pale as she approached the driver's side. I had always heard of beads of perspiration, but I had never seen them until that moment. Her breathing became almost a pant as she contemplated putting the car into drive. I finally coaxed her to put it into gear, and she drove a bit on that little stretch of asphalt surrounded by nothingness. There was not going to be improvement with time. There would never be another time when she would drive. I drove her home and put the car back into the garage.

The years passed quickly in Tonkawa. Although I was the seventh pastor in a ten-year period, I had become the longest-tenured pastor in the history of the church. With that long tenure of five years I was one of the pastors with seniority in town, and it was my turn and my duty to serve as president of the Ministerial Alliance. Each month the pastors would gather over coffee to discuss the same never-ending problem of lacking a clearing house strategy for dealing with those who were called "transients." Many of them were professional grifters who went from church to church asking for money on some pretense. A story I heard more than once involved having to make an unexpected trip to Nebraska for a funeral. After all, who could deny someone gas money when his mother had just died?

In my last and final pastorate one of the two best scammers was the farmer-looking young man in tall rubber boots who said his pickup had just run out of gas on the highway near our church. He was pulling a cattle trailer, he said, and the truck and trailer and poor cattle were left stranded on the highway unless I could give him $20 for gas. I was in the middle of a meeting, so how could I refuse? Of course he would come back very soon to pay me back.

Another local man would come by the church from time to time and ask for $10 for a few gallons of gas. Our church was located about five miles from the nearest gas station, so he used a gallon of gas coming out to us and going back to Sedalia. One time when I gave him the $10, he promised to pay me back. Some months passed, and there was William once again about to ask for money.

I quickly said, "William! You came back to pay me back just like you promised."

I had caught him by surprise, and he was a bit dumbfounded. He left with an uncertain look on his face. I thought that he might not come again, since I had gotten the better of him. One Sunday he came and endured my preaching during a Sunday service. Afterwards, he approached two of our deacons to ask for money. Somehow, I had managed to get away early that Sunday, but the deacons had the kindness and the presence of mind to send him to my house. I turned him down flatly. He had used an additional gallon of gas to get to my house which was ten minutes further from the church.

That was the last time I saw William, but only a few months passed before I heard that he had swindled an older man with dementia. He conned the poor victim into buying him a pickup truck. He had upped his game. The son of the swindled senior was a parishioner of mine. I alerted the family of his con, and the family took measures to protect their father.

On Sundays I was almost always the last one to leave after the morning worship service, and the last thing I did was to return my Bible to my office, at which time, very often, the phone would ring. My wife would be waiting in the car, and someone would call trying to catch the pastor to tell a tale of woe designed to tug at the heartstrings of the pastor—or to get the pastor quickly to dole out $50 just so he could go to lunch with his family.

Once I was caught in the church kitchen for just such a call. The situation which the woman described was the horrific car crash of her mother. The injured woman was taken by life-flight to St. Luke's Hospital in Kansas City, and the poor daughter needed to follow in her own car. She had no gas and no money for gas!

After thirty-five years in the pastorate, I had heard it all. I was pretty hard to shock, and I had become a bit jaded in response to all the lies told to me to stir my heartstrings and loosen my purse strings.

While I kept the woman on hold, I pushed the button on the phone for the other line so I could call the hospital. I asked if there had been a life-flight that morning. There had not been. The woman was lying to me, and she was very nearly successful in her con. Every pastor hears similar sad tales and has to determine which, if any, are the truth.

At the Tonkawa Ministerial Alliance meeting one day, an older pastor, Paul Mattox, offered guidance in our endless month-to-month discussions of how to deal with such scammers. Paul declared that he would rather err on the side of generosity than deny a deserving person's request. He rightly stated that we would all stand before the Judgment Seat of Christ to answer for the things done in our days here on earth.

We were all nodding our heads when the Methodist pastor said that just one week after he had moved to Tonkawa from Enid, a familiar-looking man came into his office to ask for benevolent help. He was, the man swore, a card-carrying Methodist. Pastor Jack was looking at him and trying to place him, and his visitor had a puzzled look on his face suggesting that he, too, was trying to figure out where he had seen Jack before. It came to both of them at the same time: he had trotted out the same line in Jack's office in Enid just the week before Jack had moved to Tonkawa. He left the pastor with the "you can't blame a guy for trying" schtick.

Before our ministry in Tonkawa, the little church had come to view itself as a training church for pastors. Sadly, the church never grew. It had doubled in size while we were there, but it still numbered under seventy on Sunday mornings. The budget rarely provided for a salary increase, even though the expenses of the young pastoral families increased every year. They treated their pastors as though they would be temporary, and in doing so, they made them temporary.

Wes and I had been in Tonkawa for five years, but we were sensing that it was time for us to seek our next place of ministry. We had wonderful friends there in Tonkawa, but our closest friends went to other churches, and there were very few children in our church that were the age of our children. We wanted our children to grow up in a vibrant church, and it was sad to see and to admit to ourselves that Tonkawa Bible Church was not going to be that vibrant and vigorous church.

I had been advised in seminary to write out any resignation letter or significant announcement such as a call to another ministry. At last that sad moment arrived when I shared with the little flock that Wes and I had decided to take a church in Iowa in the town of Eagle Grove. While there are always some or several families glad to see the pastor move on to the next assignment, the church, as a whole, was genuinely sad to see us go. The day before we moved from Tonkawa the church held a farewell lunch in our honor.

In my early days as a pastor, I was driving the seven miles north to Blackwell, and most likely I was going to the hospital to visit Wanda Gillispie. The sun was still low in the sky, and that may have been why I noticed it. The house was far enough from the road to leave a fair-sized front yard. The driveway to the left of the house also led to a barn with a sagging roof. The front porch was broken through with some boards in two pieces with jagged ends, and the railing had rungs that had long before gone AWOL. Paint was still clinging to the crevices in the rounds that had been machined and turned, and they still held up the roof of the porch. In the roof itself there were holes visible from the road, and in the common and furious Oklahoma thunderstorms the water must have poured into the house with a steady stream.

What caught my eye was the windmill. Every farm had to have a windmill in the days before electric pumps, and this windmill had been battered by many a storm. It was snaggle-toothed, and the few surviving blades were rusted and bent. In front of the windmill was an old tricycle tractor, maybe a Farmall, or a Massey-Ferguson, or an Oliver, or a Minneapolis-Moline. The front tires were flat, and there was a tin can covering the upright exhaust pipe.

This house had once been a home, and, no doubt, a family lived there with all the bustling activity of a farmer, his wife, and their several children. The boys had once hauled hay and slopped hogs, and the girls had helped their mother with the milking and had gathered eggs and churned butter. The children complained when they had to pick the garden, and the boys had sour dispositions when everyone had to sit for hours on the front porch rubbing their fingertips raw while shelling peas and beans. To get the family through the winter on the plains of Oklahoma, they needed to fill the few hundred jars they kept in the cellar.

Perhaps one night when the moon was high and full, a car that looked like it was from an old movie may have crept to a stop on the gravel of the driveway. The driver turned off the headlamps as he turned in, and then a young gentleman dashed around the car to open the front passenger door for his sweetheart. He closed it as silently as possible. Hand in hand they swung their arms as they walked toward the house, and then they quietly lingered on the porch for that long goodnight—until the porch light flickered on and off again a couple of times.

Every time I drove past this old abandoned and ramshackle place, I mentally transposed it to the other side of the road so that when the sun was in my mental photograph of it, I could envision the Sun going down in the west. It was the photograph that I always intended to take. I never did.

For of all sad words of tongue or pen,
The saddest are these: "It might have been!"[45]

And today, I do not pass a ragged windmill without thinking of that place and the painting that I would like, one day, to paint. The painting would be entitled: "Day Is Done."

---

[45] John Greenleaf Whittier, "Maud Muller," Poetry Archive, Accessed August 18, 2022, http://www.poetry-archive.com/w/maud_muller.html.

Chapter Thirteen

"Displaced Southerners"

Twice in our five years in Oklahoma the little church had almost doubled in size. Each time it doubled, the families that were new to us were in their child-rearing years as we were. Every couple of years, one or two of the young families in the church were transferred away by Conoco, and with each transfer we grew a bit discouraged. Our dream was to have young families for our young family—to have children in the church for our children. I sent word to the placement office at Dallas Seminary that I felt it was time for us to consider other places of ministry.

One weekend in the middle of winter we flew as a family to Des Moines for a visit to Eagle Grove, Iowa. On the Friday night of our visit, the chairman of the elders came to pick us up from the parishioner's home in which we were staying. Morrie Smith walked through the snow and whisked four-year-old Nathaniel up in his arms and carried him from the door of Blondeen Kolbo's house to the passenger's side, rear door of his car. Wes and I were already in the car on our own with Anna, and as Morrie was walking around the back of his car to the driver's seat, Nathaniel proclaimed: "I like that man!"

Morrie's eyes twinkled when he was with children. Instead of Superintendent of Schools, he should have been a kindergarten teacher. He missed his calling. We met the other elders and their wives that night, and there was an energy and a vision of which we wanted to be a part.

On Saturday morning there was a men's breakfast at The Family Table, the coffee shop of Eagle Grove. That evening we gathered with the church of some 60 people to celebrate the birthday of one of the flock. John Neibergall was the emcee that night, and so it fell to him to lead what must have been a North-Central Iowa rendition of a song that had been familiar to me in the past: "Happy Birthday."

Apart from his having, I think, the most genial personality of anyone I have ever known, he was least qualified at that moment to be a leader. I am sad to say that John Neibergall is not musically gifted. John was a journalist and was the publisher of the local newspaper. His next career was that of university professor. I do not exaggerate when I say that he is that most talented person I have ever known, and that he could have done anything he wanted to do—business, medicine, politics, ministry, teaching many subjects at any level, even . . . well, as I think about it, he couldn't have been a carpenter, or a mechanic, or an electrician, or a farmer, or a prize-fighter. I suppose there really were not that many things for which he was suited, except for those involving the intellect and the personality. I guess what I am trying to communicate is that he was not a song leader.

The next morning we gathered in a rented hall with the body that was Grace Bible Church. It was a church that did not own property or a building. When it came my time to speak, I remember reflecting on the culture shock to our little family as we ventured that far north—just 70 miles from Minnesota, the state in which I had worked one SUMMER! We had come to enjoy a good snow in Oklahoma, but there the snow knew when it had worn out its welcome. In northern Iowa the temperature took our breath, and snow was just another part of life. Still, the biggest cultural shock for me had to be that "Happy Birthday" was sung to a different tune, at least when John Neibergall led it!

April came, and it was time to move. No help with moving expenses had been offered, and yet I had accepted the call to the church in Iowa. How could I pull this off? My poor parents, again, were willing to help us make the move. This time it required a U-Haul truck, and Dad, a professional driver, was just the guy! But how would we pay for it?

I walked, hat in hand, to the office of the president of the First National Bank of Tonkawa. I had visited my tennis buddy, John Birch, on several occasions when I would just stop by to chat. That morning as I went in, I had no assurance that I could qualify for a loan of $500. We had paid cash for our first car. I never had borrowed money before, except for a small loan for a used car. I sat down across the desk from John, and I felt terribly small and insignificant. Vulnerable. If he did not grant the loan, what would we do? We had no more money than the money for our next week's groceries.

I asked John if I could borrow the money. He said to me, "I don't want to give you a loan to help you move out of town." My heart sank, and I became a bit defensive. Had I heard him correctly? He didn't think that I would be a good risk if I borrowed the money and then moved away! There was more than a moment of discomfort and misunderstanding. I felt flush. My words must not have made sense to him: "Well, I would have a reputation to protect there as well."

He then produced the papers of the loan application. I filled them out and pushed them back across the desk, still feeling like I had failed in life. How could this have been? I was 32 years old. Others of my friends had jobs that paid salaries with benefits and a 401(k), whatever that was.

I had paid my way through college, and I had finished college with enough money in the bank to have paid cash for a car and to have made a small down payment on a house. Instead of those first steps my peers were making, I had spent all of my savings on a graduate degree. I had done roofing and concrete work to make ends meet during my first pastorate in Tonkawa, but my tiny salary could not even cover a move to a place that might make a better life for us—better financially, that is.

Of course, I had completely misunderstood my friend the bank president, John Birch. He was saying that he hated to see me move and hated to be the facilitator of that move away from him and his family. It was actually a kind sentiment, but I was so insecure at that meeting that I could not imagine anyone was offering any uplifting words. They would have had to have reached pretty low to lift me up! He granted the loan, and we rented the U-Haul truck.

That was how we moved to Iowa, and then the Lord provided another loan from Wes's parents to make a down payment on our first home. We started our new life in the North, and eventually, somehow, we paid off those two loans.

Benjamin Franklin put these words in the mouth of Poor Richard in *The Way to Wealth*: "Three removes is as bad as a fire."[46] He meant, of course, that if one moved three times, the damage done to one's household goods was equal to that which a fire might do. On that move I lost my journals and poetry from my high school and college days. To this day, the sole surviving poetry which I wrote in college is what I published in the literary journal of Mississippi College.

On our first complete day in Eagle Grove when we were setting up our furniture, I heard a crashing sound and ran into the dining room to see a shelf in our cabinet as it spontaneously and inconsiderately turned at a forty-five-degree angle and allowed, one by one, ten heavy pewter plates to drop upon my grandmother's lovely, green Depression Glass tray. It splintered into thousands

---

[46] Benjamin Franklin, *Benjamin Franklin: the Autobiography and Other Writings*, ed. L. Jesse Lemisch, (New York: A Signet Classic, 1961), 191–92.

of shards, and the hutch surface was dented by the crash and the weight of those falling plates. This hutch had been my gift to Wes upon my graduation from seminary— a gift reflecting my appreciation for all of her hard work helping me to pay for the four years of seminary.

The first weeks in Eagle Grove were like those of anyone moving into a new town and home. I needed to place deposits for gas and electricity and water, and since I had moved out of state, I needed insurance for the car and the house. One morning I went into the insurance office of Jana Amdahl, who was also the mayor of Eagle Grove. I spoke to her receptionist and then stood while I waited.

After a few minutes, another customer came in. He was about my height but outweighed me by fifty pounds. His overalls over his t-shirt suggested to me that he was not a fireman or an insurance salesman. As soon as I saw him, I was transported back to my days selling dictionaries door-to-door for two summers while I was in college. After my first year of college, I had worked in Illinois and Missouri.

Selling dictionaries for eleven weeks and seventy-five hours a week allowed me to save enough money for my second year of college. At the end of that school year, I had $100 (over $750 in today's dollars) left as seed money for my second summer on the "book field" as it was called.

After my second year of college, I drove my old 1964 Ford to St. James, Minnesota. For one month I lived in an old hotel that provided cheap accommodations to penniless persons such as myself. The second month I lived in New Ulm, again, in a seedy hotel that was of the sort that had weekly and monthly rates. The third month I was in Olivia, Minnesota, staying in the garage apartment of Mrs. Roy Palmlund, a dear and matronly lady who not only housed me but also graciously fed me.

I was nearing the end of the summer on the book field. On my last call of the day I drove down a driveway into a grove of trees. I had come to identify such a grove as the shelter for a house out in the wild and wintery country in Minnesota. Every farm had a grove of evergreens that gave the illusion of protection from the wicked winds of winter.

As a salesman, I got out of my car and went directly up to the door with an air of confidence.[47] I would leave shortly with somewhat less confidence. As the farmer's wife cordially invited me into the kitchen, I saw the cab door of a big John Deere open, and out came her husband. He was in overalls and a t-shirt, and on his head was the typical farmer's bill cap with his favorite brand of corn seed advertised on it.

I knew that I should not begin the sales presentation until the entire audience was present, and so the farmer's wife and I chatted. I am sure most of the conversation was in answer to the usual query: "Where in the world are you from?" I was very obviously from the South; my accent betrayed me. After a few minutes, the kitchen door opened. I had set my satchel with my dictionaries on a counter on the opposite side of the room from the kitchen door. The dusty and burly farmer coming into the room

---

[47] I was confident. It had been just a few days since I had sold enough in one day to earn about $1,250 in 2022 dollars. It was my best day of sales in two summers of work.

was little taller than I, but he had a barrel-chest, and his arms had the muscles of a Silverback Gorilla. As he came in, I walked toward him smiling and introducing myself. He took my outstretched hand in his, and he slung my 155 pounds across the room towards the door from which he had entered. He doubled up his fists and moved towards me, with clenched jaw and fists, and through gritted teeth he sputtered and hissed and threatened: "I haven't worked all day in the fields just to come home and have to listen to a *&$$$^^$#^%&%$^&^*&&^%&%^$@#$ salesman." Having talked to four to five thousand people at the door, I had become adept at reading situations and people. I perceived that this was not going to be a sale!

Quietly and soothingly I moved my outstretched hands up and down and said, "Just let me get my books, and I'll leave," and I took a couple of steps toward them. The books were, of course, behind him then, since he had thrown me across the room. He moved toward me with his arms and fists pumping and saliva seeping and spewing through his tight-clenched teeth.

"Just let me get my books, and I'll leave," I said again. He settled down somewhat and lowered his fists. I moved across the room in front of him, picked up my books, and went to my car. I shook and trembled most of the way back to town.

And there in Eagle Grove in the office of the First Lady of Insurance was someone who seemed to be that farmer's brother—the same overalls and the same seed corn hat. He swiveled his neck slowly and looked in my direction from a few feet away. It looked as though I was about to meet someone who might be a prospect for my church.

His lips barely moved, and he grunted out the words with an undertone of distrust: "Who are you?"

I took his not too jovial or jocular greeting to be an invitation to introduce myself. His hands were clasped across his chest and inside the top part of his overalls beneath the straps, so instead of seeking to shake his hand, I merely said, "Hi, I'm Eddie Brown. I'm the new pastor of Grace Bible Church."

Endeavoring to suppress his fascination and interest, he replied, "Huhhmmnnnh," and looked away.

A week or two passed, and we needed some item from the hardware store. I went downtown to the Coast-to-Coast Hardware store on Broadway. I had found the item I was seeking and was at one of the two cash registers with the proprietor. When the phone rang, his wife answered it at the other cash register about 15 feet away. She covered the mouthpiece of the phone and excitedly said to her husband, "Mike, it's that lady from Mississippi!"

Think of that coincidence: Wes had called at the precise moment I was in the store so I could discover that a southern accent was noticeable in the place where people sounded to me like they were from "MINNEsohTUH."

It was about that time that I noticed that the accent of many of the people I was meeting was very similar to that of a radio personality I had heard for some years: Paul Harvey of Chicago. After we had lived in Eagle Grove for some months, ninety miles north of Des Moines, I came to notice that their television news team sounded a bit "southern" to me compared to the accents of the Minnesota-sounding people in Wright County, Iowa.

Chapter Fourteen

____

"It's a 'Buht'!"

One of the local Eagle Grove dentists, Dr. Michael Moffitt, called one day to say we should transplant some ash trees from a ditch outside of town. Saturday afternoon came, and he stopped by with the suitable vehicle for tree transporting. We went out by the cemetery west of town.

While we were digging up trees in the right of way alongside the highway, Mike told me about the times in high school when he would throw a sheet over himself and try to scare young couples who were looking for a secluded place on a Saturday night. The spook would make an appearance in the cemetery; a car would crank and peel out; and soon other cars would come back to try to catch a sight of the mysterious ghost.

We dug up half a dozen ash trees and took three to his house in town. He and Reba and the three boys lived in a beautifully decorated Victorian house south of downtown on the main road into Eagle Grove. We pulled up in back and began digging holes for his three trees. When they were planted, we were off to my house. I had a small lot, so it's a good thing two out of the three didn't survive the transplant.

What I write next is no spoof but a virtual verbatim and accurate, blow-by-blow rehearsal of our argument. No fooling! As we were digging and filling the dirt back in with our tools, Mike said, "Put a little more dirt around the roots." The way he pronounced the word, it sounded like "ruhtz."

I declared, "It's not 'ruhtz.' It's 'rOOts.'"

"rOOts! It's not 'rOOts.' It's 'ruhtz.' What's that up there on top of your house?"

I still had a lot of the South in me, and I replied: "It's a 'rOOf.'"

He shot back: "It's not a 'rOOf.' It's a 'ruhf.' What's that on the end of your leg?" He thought he had me then when I said what he wanted me to say.

"It's a foot. What's that ON your foot?" I asked about his boot.

He grinned with his patented toothy grin and said, "It's a 'buht.'"

Of course, neither of us budged as each presented his proof for his pronunciation, but I still say foot the way he said it, and he still says boot the way I say it, and I say roof the way he said it, and roots, for me, still rhymes with shoots. I shook some dirt on the roots and smiled and smirked. After all these years, the issue is moot. There is no more room for discussion.

"It's a 'buht.'" Ha!

That wasn't the only argument I ever had with Mike, but it was one we both enjoyed. One weekend we had visitors from our first church back in Oklahoma: Dr. and Mrs. Craig (Kayla) Evans. Craig and I were out for a walk down Broadway, going east toward town, and we were walking on the sidewalk on the north side of the street. Mike and Reba were out for a ride, and when he saw me, he pulled across the wide street and pulled alongside of us on the wrong side of the street for a car going east. He rolled down his window, and Craig and I turned to greet them. I said loudly to Craig, "This is the guy I was telling you about—the guy that drives me crazy!" Mike's chin went up with pride, and that same self-satisfied grin of his flashed with his perfect dentist teeth. There may have been nothing Mike enjoyed more than a good argument, but he once confessed that he liked to argue with me so he could see Wes's claws come out in my defense. Wes and he have some similarities in their personalities. That's all I will say about that except that this would be a good time to say how much I love my wife.

As I was leaving church one Sunday, Vance Nelson, the local policeman, pulled up in front of the community center we rented for our services. He motioned me over. He told me that the neighbor of one of my troubled parishioners had seen the man bullying his wife. He forced her into their car, and he sped away with her and the children. We went together to speak to the man. How many times did I go to confront a man who had bullied his wife?

Vance Nelson was a kind man who made a show of his agnosticism. On two occasions he used the same outrageous phrase in my presence when I was with a gathering of the local pastors. He did love to shock! He occasionally would come by my office to visit, and we had several contacts concerning the local bully.

Vance was probably some twenty-five years older than I was, so the time in life for a series of surgeries came to him before it came to me. After one of his surgeries, he was very slow to recover and was off of work for a couple of months. I went by his home to visit him one day. He invited me to sit with him on his front porch. As we sat to talk, he told me that he admired the church that I pastored. He said that he had always told himself that if he ever wanted to build a house, he would join my church first. Our church members took care of one another, and a number of carpenters and craftsmen were counted among our growing numbers.

Our little family lived on the street that led to the middle school, and the speed limit was accordingly set. As school was just about over one day, a flashy red Camaro sped by. I thought of the children who, any moment, would be crossing the streets. In the Camaro were four of the town toughs, all of them about to be out of high school one way or another. I yelled out, "Slow down!" I got into my car and pulled out of the driveway. As I went toward downtown, I noticed that the red Camaro was following me close on my tail. I had angered them, and they wanted a confrontation. I drove to the police station and pulled up in front of it. They roared off with four hands extended from the windows and not with signs of good will.

A few weeks later near the center of town there were gunshots on a weekend night. The red Camaro was present. A few weeks more passed, and somehow, I managed to meet the driver of the car. He was likely the owner of the gun. We talked occasionally, and I invited him to church. He never visited the church, but he came to youth group a few times. A youth retreat was coming up, and I invited him to attend that. He said that he would.

Late one afternoon, the red Camaro pulled into my driveway. Out hopped the young man who once had been so threatening. He told me that he had dropped out of high school and was joining the Army. He was there to tell me why he would not be able to go on the youth retreat. He was off to boot camp. That was my last contact with him.

There are times when we are used by the Lord just to plant the seed of the Gospel.[48] This was one of those times.

---

[48] The Apostle Paul speaks in 1 Corinthians 3:5–9 about the way the Lord uses each of us for differing ministries in order to share with others the Good News of the forgiveness of sin that He offers to us through the sacrificial work of Jesus when He died for our sins. One plants, another waters the seed, but the Lord causes life to spring from the Seed of the Word of God. 1 Peter 1:23–25 touches on the Gospel message as Seed for new life to spring up from spiritual death (Eph. 2:1–5).

Chapter Fifteen

"L.C., That's Me!"

I suppose I had been pastoring in Eagle Grove for a
few months when a somewhat unusual person visited
Grace Bible Church.[49] When visitors come, sometimes
they are giving the church a look with a view to joining
the ministry. Other times, they may be coming to find out
what the new pastor is like. This visitor, I believe, was in
the latter category.

He was a man of average size, and he could have had
an average appearance, but the size, really, was the only
thing average about L.C. Spencer. I met him after the
service, and, to be truthful, I was a bit wary of him. He
must have been sixty years of age or nearly that, and he
came alone. I believe he was a widower at the time. His

---

[49] Near the end of my time at Grace Bible Church, we joined The
Evangelical Free Church of America. Today the church is named Grace
Church of Eagle Grove.

brown hair had what has been called a "wide part," and he was wearing overalls, as he did every other time I saw him. The overalls usually covered a plaid shirt. His nose was slightly pointed, and he was always ready to break out into a smile.

What set him apart from other visitors to our church was the fact that when children came around, he would don fake plastic glasses with eyeballs that popped out on a spring and jiggled in front of his face and around his nose. On his first visit he was handing out religious paraphernalia and tracts. As a careful pastor, I examined the tracts to make sure they were orthodox, but all the children went home with items like a blue, plastic coin-looking piece that had on it the words "Round Tuit." He explained that these should be given to people we invited to church who said that they would come "when they got around to it." Ahhh! Clever. And then there was the pencil that had an eraser on both ends. Printed on the side of the pencil were the words: "Life without Jesus is just like this pencil. There's no point to it!" Once again, clever.

He lived some ten miles out in the country to the east of town and had a Clarion, Iowa, address. I found the house—right beside a steel business out in the country. No one answered the door of the house, so I started looking for the way into the big metal building. When I found it, I went in. There was L.C.

I said, "L.C." He said, "L.C., that's me!" And every time I ever called him on the phone, both of those greetings were repeated. L.C. was never a regular attender of our church, but he started to come virtually monthly, and he ceased to be unusual to me. He was just kind. He was a generous and Christ-centered man who loved to share Jesus with those who did not know Him.

It wasn't long before L.C. told me he had bought a new 15-passenger van, and it was available to churches for mission trips, for transporting kids to camp, or for any church activity. We would pay the gas, and he would have it serviced and insured and ready for pickup. Then he got two more vans just like the first one. And then he bought an old but reliable school bus, and he would make himself available to drive that when it was needed.

A kind friend sent our family some money for our children, and that gave me the opportunity to build a sandbox with a ladder for the fort above it. Every fort needs a slide, so I thought I would see what L.C. Spencer's Steel Company might have to offer. I told him what I was planning, and he pointed to a piece of steel leaning on the wall and said, "What about that piece?"

It was stainless steel, 8 feet by 4 feet. I said, "That would be great! How much is that?"

"Oh, nothing. Just take it." It was to him a piece of scrap metal, but it was exactly what I was looking for.

"No, L.C. I want to pay for it. How much?"

"Ohhhh. How about twenty bucks?" I thought that was a bit steep, but I opened my wallet and gave him a twenty. I wanted to pay my way, after all.

When I got it home, a friend came over to see how the project was progressing. He had worked with steel when he lived in Chicago. He said, "Wow! Where'd you get that?"

"From L.C."

"What did *that* cost?"

"Annnhhh, it was $20."

"Whoa. That's worth at least a hundred bucks!"

That's L.C.

A year or so passed, and our house was needing attention. When we had moved to Eagle Grove in 1985, the Farm Crisis was beginning, and housing prices were joining hands across the neighborhood and leaping into a sinkhole. We bought the house for $24,000, but it had sold five years earlier for $42,500. We lived in Wright County for five and one-half years, and during that time the county lost some 15% of the population due to high unemployment. Crop prices were low; equipment and fuel costs were high; and the price of land had escalated dramatically. The *Des Moines Register* featured a story about farmers who were committing suicide as their machinery was repossessed or when their family farms were sold at auction.

Our house happened to be the first house to have been built in Eagle Grove. It occupied the highest point in the town of 4,200 persons. We were told there was one house that was older, but it had been built in the country and had been moved into town. Our house was built in 1873 by Judge Sumner B. Hewett, Jr. It was small but attractive, and featured a second story with a flat, but slightly sloped, roof. It was said that Judge Hewett had been able to stand atop his house and see Native Americans paddling canoes on the river a mile to the west. You can't believe everything that you hear, but there was no denying that the house was old.

We lived on the *hill*, and that hill was sometimes referred to by its detractors as "Snob Hill." Our neighbor south of us had the title "Dr." His brother on the east corner had the same title. Across the street from Dr. Emerson was Dr. Varland, one of the two town dentists. The doctors Emerson were veterinarians. Half a block to the west lived our medical doctor, and one of the elders in our church, Dr. George Hogenson.

When we moved into our house, Wes met Dr. Wayne Emerson, our neighbor to the south. He told her, "Tell your husband not to buy a snow blower." It had not occurred to this Mississippi boy that I might need a snow blower. I am not sure I had ever heard of a snow blower.

When I was growing up in Mississippi, we occasionally had snow—sometimes as much as four inches in a single year. Once we had seven inches. More frequently we had ice. When we lived in Dallas, once or twice snows shut down the city and the seminary. That's when the students went from our apartments across the street to the big lawn of the seminary for snowball fights. With bread bags[50] over the socks on our hands for mittens, and rubber bands around our ankles to keep the bread bags *on* our feet, we went into battle. The snow was usually quite wet.

In Oklahoma, the snows were more frequent and deeper. During one magical snow in February of 1980, I awoke to the sound of thunder. I was quite puzzled. I got up at 2:00 AM and looked outside. It was snowing a heavy snow, and there was lightning and thunder in a dazzling display. I have observed thunder and lightning with snow only once more, and it was here in Missouri.

---

[50] We saved plastic bags such as bread bags. After all, you never knew when you might need one to cover the socks you wore on your hands as mittens! This was something we had done in Mississippi in my youth.

During our first winter in Eagle Grove, by my careful measurement, we had fifty-two inches of snow. Eagle Grove had a city ordinance that mandated the removal of snow from sidewalks by 9:00 AM. Dr. Emerson made the offer to me that I could use his snow blower if I first cleaned his driveway and his sidewalks. His driveway was fairly large, and that took some time, but his sidewalks led to my sidewalks, so they were easy to do. Our first snow in Iowa was on November 7, 1985, and it was a seven-inch snow. Dutifully, I arose at 6:00 AM and proceeded to clean the Emersons' driveway and then mine. I then drove downtown to my office to clean that sidewalk.

Our church's curmudgeonly landlord, Kermit Fjetland, lived next door to the space our church plant rented for an office. He operated a shoe repair shop in a space lined with well-made shelves. Those shelves, in another day and time, had displayed shoes for sale. I shoveled his sidewalk when I did the church office sidewalk. Occasionally I would be there early enough to see the big John Deere tractor rolling through downtown with a dump truck just in front of it to one side so it could receive the snow propelled by the huge snow blower and augur attachment. A few quick passes and a massive amount of snow was removed. This southern boy had never imagined such equipment.

By the end of the month the first blizzard was forecasted. It lived up to expectations and brought us 14 inches driven by 25 MPH winds. The snow piled up against the elementary school and the middle school, both just two blocks from us. We could walk up the drift to go on top of the schools. As the snow was beginning to fall on that Saturday afternoon, we put our two children into our little front-wheel-drive Subaru wagon and went to look around. We had never seen a whiteout before. We drove carefully to the edge of town until we could not see ten feet in front of us. I tried to back the car up. The tires spun. The car was stuck. I said aloud what I thought: "I think I have *maaaaaade* a mistake." Nathaniel panicked and said loudly and scoldingly, "Daddy!" I got out to push, and Wes drove us backwards. We made it home for the real storm. The next morning after the wind had howled all night, the snow was level with the edge of our porch. We had never seen anything like that. I had put the car in the garage, so when 6:30 AM came and the snow was beginning to subside, I went out to experience a -37° wind chill index for my first time. I was shoveling the drift by the garage for an hour and a half before I had displaced enough snow to open the garage door. Just then Joe and "Slip," two of our deacons, showed up in a four-wheel drive pickup with a huge snow blower in the back.[51] In five minutes they had thrown the snow halfway to Minneapolis. I could then go into the house, dry off from the sweat I had produced under my heavy coat, thaw the icicles in my mustache, and get ready for church. With a modicum of pride, we never cancelled church services— even when the Lutherans did!

---

[51] The alert reader might wonder why I did not use Dr. Emerson's small snow blower. That is the reason. It was small and was not a two-stage snow blower which propelled the snow through the air with the greatest of ease!

On the Saturday night while I was keeping watch as the storm howled, I checked the basement, and in one area, I felt a very cool breeze. I put my hand up to the brickwork that was the foundation. Air was coming in, and in the light of my flashlight, I could see snow! Mondays were my days off, and almost every Monday for five years, I added mortar to the bricks, added insulation wherever I could, scraped or painted in one place or another. After a leak upstairs, I had to tear out the plaster ceiling and replace it with sheetrock. There were bats in the four attic storage spaces upstairs, and occasionally they made their way downstairs to add zest to life. The roof leaked; the plumbing was ancient; the windows had to be reglazed; and if the house was not in need of attention, the free-to-a-good-home clothes dryer we had brought from Oklahoma was breaking down every few months. I didn't have money for repairmen, so I learned quite a bit.

Another project was looming, but I had some ideas on how I was going to take care of it. The front porch had rotted out in places, and it had to be replaced. The problem was that there was a walkout balcony that overhung the porch. The access to it was out a door from the upstairs bedroom. The porch was of tongue-in-groove boards, and on the porch were three, 12-inch columns, each on a wooden pedestal.

Even then I enjoyed figuring out how to accomplish tasks like this one, so I went to L.C. and asked him if I could "borrow" some steel.

He said, "Sure. What do you need it for?"

I described the project and told him I needed a piece that was 18 feet long and then I needed two pieces that were about ten feet long.

"Okay. How are you going to keep the pieces of steel together?"

"Hmmmm. I hadn't thought about that."

"Well, I can weld some pieces together for you."

"Oh, wow. That would be great."

"How are you going to jack up the roof over the porch? What are you going to use for jacks?"

"Hmmmm. I've seen something called 'bottle jacks.'"

"That might not be big enough. Tell you what. I have some railroad jacks, and I can bring those over."

After a few days, he pulled up in front of my house with the steel he had welded together so that the vertical steel pieces could be set securely in place atop the huge jacks. The jacks weighed about one hundred pounds, and their capacity was some twenty tons, I believe. On one end of the ten-foot vertical pieces he had welded a pedestal to sit upon the jack. On the underside of the eighteen-foot horizontal piece he had welded a six-inch-long sleeve on each end. Into these sleeves the vertical pieces could fit and be held securely in place. In a few moments, L.C. had jacked up the overhang to hold it in place while the columns were removed and while the floor was replaced.

A contractor in the church also had taken pity on me. He arrived the next morning, and he showed me how to nail tongue-in-groove decking in place. Superintendent of Schools and chairman of our elders, Morrie Smith, was the next person with a measure of pity in his heart. We went to the school shop to produce some one-foot square pedestals for the eight-foot columns. The round columns were made of rounded wooden pieces that were glued together, and the pieces had begun to separate. Morrie had an idea about how to correct that. He put three metal bands around each column with a band near the base, one at the center, and a third towards the top of each column. I primed and painted the columns and set them on the pedestals on top of the new porch. The roof supports were taken down, and L.C. took the "borrowed steel" away.

I came to think of L.C. Spencer as a man who loved Jesus and who served His people. The last time I heard from him was a year or so after we moved to Sedalia. L.C. was driving to Missouri to visit a Christian youth camp near the city of Eldon. He must have seen that he was going to pass near my home. He called ahead to see if I was going to build another fort for my children. I said that I was hoping to do so. He asked if I needed a little piece of scrap metal for a slide. I said that I did. A few days later, he arrived in his van with a ten-foot-by-four-foot piece of stainless steel. I built the slide, and when the lake behind my house froze solid, the fun would begin. My children would climb the ladder to the six-foot-high platform atop the fort and slide down the slide on their plastic toboggans. They would shoot over the snow and out onto the frozen lake.

We had been in Eagle Grove for over four years, but it was becoming more obvious to us that our time there was drawing to an end. We were really a little too far north for our comfort. The trip back to our beloved Mississippi families was twenty or more hours. As our parents aged, we longed to be closer for the next phase of life. We had met many wonderfully gracious and loving souls in Iowa, and our children had friends and companions as we had hoped, but we were still a few years away from finding that place that came most to feel like . . . home.

Chapter Sixteen

"You Always Say That!"

Our little family was, by and large, happy in Eagle Grove, Iowa. True, we were struggling to make ends meet on what was a meager salary. One morning Anna was walking across the dining room. She was about to walk two blocks to the elementary school where she was a second-grade student. I said to her these words: "Be careful." She stopped; she turned; she cocked her curly-haired head sideways, and she said, "You always say that!"

Hmmm!

That day I was driving to a meeting about two hours away. I was listening to a cassette tape of the preaching of Chuck Swindoll. I don't know what he said, but I stopped the tape and said aloud to God and myself: "I need to move!" I still had been thinking about what Anna had said. Why would I say those words? Why would they be so much a part of my consciousness? Why, those were the words that my father had said to me. All of my life I had been careful. It was time for me to take the risk rather than doing the comfortable and safe thing and remaining where I was.

It was the fall of 1989. A few weeks later, I attended a pastors' conference at Dallas Seminary. I flew back through Chicago and called Wes from the airport. She said that friends[52] of ours in Oklahoma City had called. They wondered if we were open to my being considered as a candidate for the senior pastor position of their thriving church. When I was back home and settled, I called them to find out details. The search committee called, and I answered a plethora of questions. We interacted for about three months. I was deciding that it was not a good fit, and they decided the same. They were a little too Baptist for me, and I was not quite Baptist enough for them.

The door had been cracked open. I had decided that I needed to move.

I called the placement office at Dallas Seminary. Six weeks later I was in touch with some church in Sedalia, Missouri, and one in Austin, Texas. And six weeks after that, I was the number two choice of the search committees in both Austin and in Sedalia. I was the number one choice in a church in North Carolina and in a church in northern Indiana. I sent out one more resume to a church in Alabama. It would have been less than four hours from our parents. It looked promising. And then I heard from Sedalia, Missouri, that their number one

---

[52] Craig and Kayla Evans.

choice had turned them down. Would I still consider it? I said that I would.

It was a hot July afternoon when four men appeared on our front porch in Eagle Grove, Iowa. Wes and I had lived there for some five years as I pastored my second church. Caleb, our third child, was born while we were there, and we had just buried our beloved first dog, Eustace. I had recently announced to the church there in Eagle Grove that I was "feeling led to seek another ministry."[53]

The Brown family in Eagle Grove

One of the men assembled on the porch had on a t-shirt decrying the abortion industry and its wholesale

---

[53] I will mention that I had been encouraged to "feel led to seek another ministry." I don't want this book to be too sanitized and unrealistically sanguine. Pastors usually use the language of "feeling led" even when they are feeling something quite different. I offer this qualification of the account in the interest of full disclosure.

slaughter of babies. Another was dressed in preppie clothes: chino slacks with a polo shirt and leather-soled loafers. A slim and fit coach was in the mix with Adidas gear, and there was a cowboy-booted farmer in Wrangler jeans. In any other context this would have been a decidedly unlikely associated group, but that afternoon they were a search committee for a church in central Missouri. They were from Sedalia.

We invited them in, and the interview began. They were staying in Fort Dodge, Iowa, the nearest city with a motel. One of them, Danny Collins, commented that one motel they had passed had listed its sterling features out front on the marquis. That motel had both air conditioning and . . . carpet! We visited for a time and then drove back to Fort Dodge for dinner. The next morning they came to our little church to hear the prospective pastoral candidate preach.

I had informed the church that we would have a search committee present that Sunday. In a church of about a hundred, it was best to be completely upfront, since there certainly could be no successful subterfuge. I did share with the search committee that I would like for them to wear the plastic glasses, big nose, and mustache type disguises so that no one would notice them. To the church I suggested that we set up a table and four chairs on the side, like a judge's table so that they could have a good view of the pulpiteer.

The following morning two others arrived from Sedalia, and following the worship service, several of our friends hosted a meal for us and the search committee in our dining room. Another interview ensued. Two days later, the chairman of the committee called to ask if I was available to candidate on a particular August weekend. I assured him that I was.

A week before that event our little family drove to see our parents in Mississippi for vacation. The week passed fast, and when Friday arrived, we roused the children at 3:00 AM and loaded them into our Chevrolet Celebrity station wagon for the 650-mile trek from Mississippi to Sedalia. The first event was the planned meeting with the chairman of the search committee at his home, but we arrived in town about 3:30 in the afternoon. There was time to tour the town blindly by ourselves. We turned down 16th Street to the east. I thought perhaps that was Sedalia's Main Street. It was not too impressive—a donut shop, a school built in the 1940s, a barber shop, and a few other assorted offices and businesses. Next, we drove out to Maplewood Church and pulled into the parking lot. The line drawing of the church building on the church stationery looked more impressive than did the smaller-than-I-imagined building in its dusty, gravel parking lot.

We had driven around enough to find the home of Jeff and Shelley McGuire down a lovely maple-tree-lined street. They and their three girls shared a modest home three blocks south of Broadway—the street which had many of the larger, stately old homes in Sedalia. Nathaniel was 9; Anna was 8; and Caleb was 21 months old. Little did we know that Anna was meeting one of her college roommates that evening. Two nights later she met another one.

Around 6:00 we went by the church again, and this time, Jeff took us inside. Maplewood Church was in the middle of a remodeling project. They were adding some seventy-five seats to the sanctuary. We met a few folks there, and then we were off to a home on Highway TT. Inside and waiting for the "ambush" were the elders and their wives.

This was the home of Norma and Jim Sumner. Jim invited us in—actually he grabbed my hand and rather pulled me into his home. He was short, stocky, and dark-complected. This one who was fond of saying that you never get a second chance to make a good first impression, well—he made quite an impression. There was a wonderful meal that I was a little too nervous to eat, and then the back-and-forth questioning involved in determining if I would be a good fit for the church and if the church would be a good fit for me. I had been up since 3:00 that morning, and I had driven twelve hours with three children.

Somewhere around 11:30, it seemed like Jim Sumner was coming alive. I would say that he was getting his "second wind," but he did not seem to have lost his first wind. Somehow, around 12:30 the next morning, we made our way back to pick up our children at the McGuires', and somewhere around 1:00 AM we fell into bed at the house where we were staying. The owners, Paul and Sondra Calvert, stayed with his parents that weekend.

The men's breakfast started at 6:30 AM, and then followed the interview with the deacons. Lunch with two couples, and then one of the couples took us around Sedalia to show us different sections of town so we could understand something of the housing market. Everything was far out of our limited reach. We would have to rent if we moved to Sedalia.

And then it happened. It was the sort of thing that is funny when someone else's kid says it to someone you don't know or to someone who is not voting on whether or not you should be hired. We were riding along with a dear older couple. Wes was in the backseat with our two younger children and the dear lady, and I was in the front seat with the kind gentleman and young Nathaniel.

It started out so nicely when Nathaniel turned around and said to the grandmotherly woman in the backseat, "I don't mean to be rude, but why do you have a mustache?" It was the same sort of feeling I had about three years earlier when he asked a man in back of us at the checkout at Target, "Are you a mean man?" Thankfully, with Nathaniel's slight speech impediment, the man had not understood what was said, but Wes and I did. Despite embarrassment and nervous laughter, the couple was kind, and they became dear friends. They loved us and our children.

That was the end of the day's planned activities. We visited one of the families in the church and then went to the Wheel-In Drive-In for a hamburger. The Wheel-In was once featured in *Southern Living* magazine and was famous for its peanut butter slathered hamburger. It was called a "goober-burger." A patron there had on a t-shirt with the only KKK insignia I have ever seen, but then, the State Fair was going on that week.

The next morning I woke up in a house that did not have a coffee maker, nor did they have coffee. I scrambled outside to get in my car to go to a service station to find coffee at 5:30 AM. I was fairly exhausted, but with the importance of the weekend and the day before me, I had slept fitfully.

Finally, we were ushered into the sanctuary for the worship service. I was guided to a small two-person pew on the stage. We followed a familiar order of worship, and then one of the elders rose to pray before the message— the message that I would deliver and the message on which my future hung. The dear man prayed. And he prayed some more. And after three or four minutes with my eyes closed for prayer, I fell asleep. Up there on the stage! Up there before the eyes of everyone who would soon vote on whether or not to call me to that ministry. I did have this in my favor: my head was in an appropriately prayerful position while I slept. Somehow, by the grace of God or a lustily loud "Amen!", I came back to life just in time to enter the pulpit.

After the service, I stood at the door and met a young couple who had just moved to Sedalia from Louisiana. Both were teachers, and he was an appropriately tall basketball coach. I thought of the irony of the church's receiving two new couples that weekend: one from Mississippi and one from Louisiana.[54]

There was a covered-dish lunch in the fellowship hall; an unscheduled afternoon; and then the meeting in the sanctuary for questions from the congregation. There were about 150 people gathered in the sanctuary, and I stood in the pulpit fielding questions from the floor. There

---

[54] I later found out that Becki and Jeff Backe had moved to Sedalia from Louisiana, Missouri!

were doctrinal questions and procedural questions and ethics questions. Some of the questions probed areas in which I knew I was weak: vision and planning. I never became that visionary pastor that every church wanted. As it turned out, I was just a plodder. One foot in front of the other repeated for thousands and tens of thousands of times. And I wasn't a quitter.

During the questioning I noticed a man and a woman on the back row on the right side. They seemed angry. Intense. The questions sprang from deep passion. Two of the questions focused on my stance on abortion. I did not think I had met either of the eager questioners during the course of the weekend to that point, but as soon as the time for questions was over, the woman came rushing up to me from the back of the church. She was smiling, and she said, "Well, do you like us?" I was taken aback. She had just been firing questions at me from a deep well of intensity. I was amused.

I thought the time had gone reasonably well, and I thought the interviews were over and that everyone had all the information needed to vote either yea or nay. I began to relax. Keith and Sherry Sumner took us over to meet another couple that night. Lo and behold, the angry man from the back row was there to welcome us into his home. He was obviously an athlete. He was an inch shorter than I was but seemed very stout. I begged the use of their bathroom shortly after we arrived. When I came out, this man was blocking my passage, standing in the hallway with his shoulders lower on one side than the other and with his hands on his hips. With no other introduction to our conversation, he said, "Well, are you man enough to be my pastor?"

I was frustrated by that time, and I blurted out, "I don't know!" Indeed, I did not know. And then I found out he was a world champion wrestler. Ohhhhh! He had been the NCAA champ at Oklahoma State University and had made the Olympic wrestling team, but President Carter boycotted the Olympics that year. I guess he was still angry about that.

We left the next morning to drive the six hours north to our home in Eagle Grove, Iowa. On Tuesday morning, Dr. Bob Boatright, the chairman of the elders, called to offer me the position. He then stated the salary they were offering.[55] I told him that I did not think we could live on that amount in Sedalia, Missouri, where the cost of living was higher than it was in rural Iowa. The following morning a counteroffer came, and I accepted that. Three weeks later we moved to Sedalia.

Our first Sunday at Maplewood Church was the 25th anniversary of the founding of the church. All of the former pastors in that twenty-five-year stretch were present to be a part of the festivities. During the lunch which followed the worship service, the wife of one of the elders received a phone call saying that her elderly mother had died. I made the announcement to the parishioners who were gathered for the meal, and I led in prayer for the comfort of those who had suffered the loss.

---

[55] The church in northern Indiana had offered both a parsonage and an additional $10,000 salary. But . . . it was 20 hours from our parents in Mississippi.

The following morning I began to get to know my secretary, Eunice Smith. Before the week was out her husband was found lifeless in their garage. I had two funerals my second week at Maplewood.

Chapter Seventeen

"Lord, Did We Step Out of Your Will?"

We were living in a rental house in the neighborhood adjacent to the church, and the house was situated beside a small lake with an island in the center. My concern when we moved in was that my toddler would walk right out into the lake. Right after the moving trucks had been unloaded, Dr. Bob Boatright asked if I wanted a fence. Within two hours there was a woven wire fence on steel t-posts in the backyard. At about 8:00 the next morning, my phone rang. I heard the name of the caller. He was the president of the homeowner's association. His charming welcome-to-the-neighborhood speech skipped all the niceties and went immediately to the words: "You have to take the fence down." I heard his name; his title; and the message. It was all over in thirty seconds.

By our second Tuesday in Sedalia, our son, Caleb, at 22 months of age, was still sick. Wes had stayed at home with him on our first Sunday in the new church. She then joined us for lunch in the fellowship hall. Caleb had had high fever through the weekend, but on the Tuesday of that difficult week he was increasingly lethargic and limp.

Dr. Bob admitted him to the hospital that afternoon. Caleb would be hospitalized for nine nights with severe pneumonia. I stayed with him one night to give Wes a break.

Several days during the first two weeks Anna came home from school crying. Had we stayed in Iowa, Anna would have learned to read and write in cursive as a third grader. At her new school at Smithton, the students in her class had learned cursive the year before—in the second grade. She was an excellent reader, but she could not read the words the teacher was writing on the blackboard. She felt terribly behind. Nevertheless, she learned cursive that week! Each night we went to the hospital to visit Caleb and Wes, and each night we had to do the homework assigned by their new teachers. I had to help them each night. I had two funerals that week as well as a parishioner in the hospital in Kansas City. Perhaps there would be time also to prepare a message for the Sunday morning and evening services.

The following week, on Monday morning, I had gotten Nathaniel and Anna to school, and I was mowing the lawn with a little, aged, twenty-inch push mower. The lawn was just over half an acre in size, and the grass had not been cut in weeks. I had gotten the kids to school; it was my day off; I had to mow. I would push the mower a few feet forward, and then the thick, damp grass would choke the mower, and I would have to pull it back a foot to let the tiny engine catch up. Over and over, forwards and back!

Around 9:00 AM, I called to check on Caleb. Wes said that she thought Caleb was dying. I left the mower in the middle of the backyard and began my drive to the hospital to see my son. As I drove, I prepared to call Ken Sheppard, my pastor, to do the funeral service for our baby.

Our stress level was as high as it had ever been. I began to wonder if, somehow, we had stepped out of the Lord's will. Was that why so many things were going wrong? "Lord, what are you trying to tell me?"

An excellent pediatrician had been monitoring Caleb's case and was daily available to give us updates on his condition. He believed Caleb had a bacterial pneumonia and had begun treating him for that. For some reason, it was Friday, the third day of Caleb's hospitalization, before bloodwork had been ordered. The pediatrician was seeking to determine whether the pneumonia was bacterial or viral. For some other unknown reason, the blood sample had not been sent on that Friday afternoon to Columbia for testing. It did not go out on Saturday. It did not go out on Sunday. It was sent to Columbia on Monday morning, Caleb's sixth day in the hospital. A full week after his admission to the hospital word came that Caleb's pneumonia was bacterial, and the doctor had been treating him with appropriate medications.

In the thirty minutes between my dismal Monday morning conversation with Wes and my arrival at the hospital, the pediatrician had come in. Caleb was beginning to respond to the medication. Despite what Wes had thought earlier, he actually was beginning to improve. Caleb was released on Thursday of that week.

The next week brought my first meeting with the elders of my new church. I didn't know what to expect. Their style of governance in the meetings and in the church was different from that of the churches I formerly had pastored. I sat in the meeting as it spun out of control. A heated discussion on a policy matter with its foundation in the interpretation of an ambiguous passage in the New Testament was the reason for the tension. By the end of the meeting, a vote was taken among the voting elders, and the vote was split.

During the course of the meeting one elder asked my opinion on the matter. I stated that I could see good reasons for both points of view. He responded, "Great, my pastor doesn't know what he thinks about this crucial issue." That was not precisely accurate, but I was trying to mediate the tensions in the room, and I certainly didn't want to start off my first elders meeting with a divided board. And yet that was just what we had.

The elder who had spoken sarcastically called the next day to ask my forgiveness, and he offered to make an apology to me in the venue of my choosing, implying he would do so before the board in the next meeting if I chose. I accepted his apology, and that was the end of it. (Well, obviously I mentioned it here.)

It was another month before I discovered a major source of division in the congregation. One of the more prominent committees was in conflict. I was more and more inclined not to unpack the nonessential boxes we had packed for our recent move to Sedalia.

Our family had finished dinner one evening when I decided to call one of the godly mentors from my seminary days in Dallas. His wife answered the phone, and I visited with her just a moment before I asked to speak to John. There was silence. "Oh, Eddie! I'm so sorry. No one called you? John died of cancer three weeks ago." I wept.

As I settled into the week-to-week schedule and rhythm of pastoring and preaching in the country just outside of Sedalia, life began to normalize. The kids gradually adjusted to their new schools, but Anna began to pray every night that she would be able to go to the little Christian school run by three couples in our church. By the second semester, "the Lord had heard her prayer," and she started going to Applewood Christian School with three of her lifelong friends. Two of them would be her roommates in college.

Chapter Eighteen

"Yes, Dear!"

One Sunday a new couple visited Maplewood Church. The gentleman was tall and slender with his hair combed back from a widow's peak, and his wife spoke with a heavy German accent. I spoke to the gentleman first since he was near the pulpit I had just left. In a few moments I learned that he was retired from the Air Force and had finished his career at Whiteman Air Force Base.[56] He had met his wife-to-be while he was stationed at Ramstein Air Force Base in Germany. He explained that he was deaf in his left ear and partially deaf in his right ear.

From the back of the church a voice called out to him: "John!"

---

[56] Whiteman Air Force Base is in Knob Noster, Missouri, about 15 miles west of Sedalia.

He put his hand up to his ear to cup the sound. Mind you, he put his hand up to his left ear, his deaf one—and he said, "Yes, Dear." He winked at me.

A visit to their home that week was instructive. I heard more of their history, but I got to know the real John and Leslie. I heard Leslie's remarkable story of the Russian invasion of her native Prussia during the Second World War. She told of how she, as a six-year-old, had given a Russian officer a severe tongue-lashing in Polish. A small crowd formed around her. He and the other junior officers found her amusing. They were there on serious business, however, because they were conscripting men to join them in their push against Nazi Germany. She used choice words—words that polite little girls didn't use, and all because they were trying to take her father from her. The officer told Leslie to tell her father to get a limb from a tree and to make a crutch. He was to limp severely and lean on the crutch. He avoided conscription, and that was the beginning of their overland flight from the Russians. Somehow her family had survived.

John's and Leslie's interactions were gruff. Indeed, John's first words to me as he "welcomed" me into their home through the front door . . . they also seemed gruff. There were arguments, disagreements, and when one would end, John would look at me, smile, and shrug his shoulders. Leslie would be frustrated that he had broken off the argument.

That was the last time I ever went to the front door. Only strangers went to the front door—not friends. A few years passed, and so did Leslie's health. They had been in Bible studies with me over a few years, and I had come to expect that at some point Leslie would object to something that I had said. We would argue back and forth for a time, and finally, I would try to exit from the argument, just as I had seen John do. Leslie enjoyed arguing. I did not. I do not.

Another visitor came to church one Sunday with his family. It was my good friend, Dr. Brett Liesemeyer. I said to Leslie, "Leslie, go and talk to Dr. Liesemeyer in German." Brett's forebears had been here to welcome the Pilgrims when they landed. "Liesemeyer" was the only German word he knew. She went to him with relish and unleashed. He looked at her with blank astonishment. Of course, she came back after me. "Auch, you knew he didn't speak Deutsch!"

One Sunday after church, Leslie and I had our longest, deepest argument. Again, something I had said in the sermon had set her off. My beliefs were basically baptistic, and one of them involves what some would call "eternal security." Others would describe it more accurately as "perseverance of the saints," as I tend to describe the experience of the genuine believer in Jesus Christ. My core belief is that if a person is truly saved, that salvation is eternal. Those genuinely saved are, as the Bible says, "born again." My belief is that when one is born again, it is unto a life which begins but never ends.

That Sunday, however, Leslie had decided that she had lost her salvation, and I believed she had not! We argued back and forth. The last parishioners had gone out one door or the other from the sanctuary, but the discussion continued. It became more and more lively and finally was positively heated. Leslie was growing intense. I had lost my patience, but, more to the point, I was out of time. My family was waiting on me, and I had to bring the discussion to a close. Again, Leslie was arguing that she had lost her salvation.

Understand what she was believing to be true about her situation: she thought that she was going to hell! She said she had lost her salvation, and I fairly yelled, "LESLIE! YOU'RE WRONG!" A smile spread across her face. She was believing that she was, indeed, saved! Hallelujah!

That, of course, was not our last argument, only our most heated.

In April of 2007, one of my parishioners called to make an appointment with me for herself and her husband. They had been attending church for about a year, and I had had lunch with her husband a couple of times. I had been a pastor for nearly thirty years, and I thought that I had heard it all. It was not easy to surprise me—or to fool me. They entered into my counseling suite outside my study. I had a hunch about what we would be discussing. I was wrong.

"Tell me what I can do for you," I said.

The young man was nervous and emotional. I had known many men who finally submitted to the ultimatum: "Either we go to counseling, or I'm leaving you."

The young woman reached for a tissue and dabbed at a tear. Her voice trembled as she said, "I've just been diagnosed with cancer."

"Oh, Suzanne, I'm so sorry. I had no idea."

"We haven't told the children yet, but to make matters worse, it's the same kind that my father had. We had his funeral last month. Six months after he was diagnosed."

In effect, she was telling me that she believed that she had six months to live. Within a month, her appearance began to change. The treatments she underwent were aggressive, but after a few months, there was no progress. Soon I did not see her at church, and when I saw her husband, he spoke in positive and upbeat terms. Her absence, however, revealed much more.

Just after Thanksgiving I was visiting with her in her home. Suzanne had not left her home in many weeks except to see her doctors. It was evident that she was nearing the end of her life. In such situations over the years I have spoken very frankly with people who know they are dying. As a pastor, I am generally welcomed to speak directly and to say what is also on their minds. I asked her if she *knew* that she knew Jesus as Lord and Savior. We talked. She wanted to have assurance of her salvation. I guided her in prayer as she made a very clear confession of faith in Jesus. She then expressed her desire to be baptized. A few days later, in the presence of her sister, her children, and her husband, I baptized her in her home.

Saturday came, and I was about to leave my study to perform a wedding. Wes called from the home of the young woman to tell me that she had slipped away that afternoon. It was 1:55 PM.

One month before this tragic death, John Robinson stopped by my office to talk. He said to me with tears in his eyes, "Pastor Eddie. I have prayed that the Lord would take the cancer away from Suzanne and that he would give it to me." Tears came to my eyes . . . that John would care so much. I told him that was a wonderful and gracious thought. The Lord, simply, does not govern His world in just that way. John understood, but his intentions and his prayer revealed the kind and tender heart of John Robinson.

We began to see Leslie less and less at church, and then she had a debilitating stroke. I couldn't imagine that she could rebound from it. I saw her in the hospital in Columbia over several weeks, and then she was transferred to a rehabilitation center there. I saw her several more times. John would visit frequently as well.

Eventually she was brought back to their home. How could John take care of her? He was developing his own physical issues. He could no longer walk in a straight line. There was a terrible tremor in his leg. One of his feet no longer functioned in a normal manner. His balance was intermittent. Still, he would lean over with one hand on the arm of Leslie's wheelchair, and with the other hand he would pull her up by a strap that went under her arms and around her back. They managed to stay in their home alone.

Leslie's condition continued to degrade. She was hospitalized in Sedalia for over a month at one point. We had the inevitable conversations about the end of life, but she had come to the point that it was what she wanted. She wanted to be released from the body that so completely had rebelled against her.

John and I began to talk about a nursing home for her. One day I took him to nearby Tipton to talk to the administrator there. He liked what he saw. It was where she lived out her final days, and it was where he spent his as well.

On one of my visits with John while he still was living in their home, he had heard from our mutual friend, Dr. Liesemeyer. John's vision was so poor he could no longer be permitted to drive. He was struggling with that news, but he let me drive him to the grocery store and pharmacy that day. His independence was all but over. One day, just as Leslie had two and one-half years before, he found a new and joyful freedom.

He was buried in a military cemetery with full military honors. I read his obituary the day of his funeral. It used familiar words describing what had happened just days before. At the age of 85, John "passed away" at Tipton Oak Manor. Of course, for us all, there comes that time when we take our last breath.

For the Christian, the Scriptures[57] speak of being "absent from the body, present with the Lord." The Apostle Paul said what is true for those who walk with Jesus: "For to me, to live is Christ; to die is gain!" Paul was saying the primary focus of all of his life was taken up with his relationship with Jesus, but at that moment of his last breath, he would gain a face-to-face experience of the presence of his Savior. That is the testimony of those who have placed their faith in the Lord Jesus Christ

---

[57] 2 Cor. 5:8 and Phil. 1:21 (AV).

as personal Savior and Lord. John had done so, and Leslie had done so.

I go back to those words most typically used as circumlocutions for death and dying: "passing" or "pass away." Die, death, dead—all are, to be sure, harsh and cold in their finality. There is something piercingly abrupt about them, and most people tend to avoid them and talk around them, as the word "circumlocution" suggests. But the words "pass away" may be more apropos today than ever before.

For the last few generations it has been customary for the elderly to reach that point of not being able to sustain life alone in their own homes. They needed care in their final years, and the "old peoples' home" was the answer for many. Their activities would be truncated. After all, even if the retirement home had a garage for their cars, they gradually drove less and less. Then, too, the homes would provide a bus for transportation to community events or to the grocery stores. Often there were church services offered in the various retirement homes, so there was one more outing each week that was curtailed.

And then the horrid virus that went round the world came at last to where we were—and to where our loved ones were in their homes for the aged and infirm. The cut-off was absolute for most of them. The homes where they had enjoyed some fellowship with others in their similar life situations suddenly became more like prisons than communities. For many, the only human contact they had for a full year was with the person bringing trays of food. That person didn't have a face. He or she came with a mask to meet them, likewise, faceless and in a mask themselves. Bright moments came when some who were blessed with a window to the outside world could see family members arrange themselves in view of the window. Perhaps they were attired in Christmas colors when the grandchildren were home with their own children or from their own lives far away. For some, voices could be heard over the phone, but some could no longer hear. And, sadly, with the gradual but hastening deterioration of the mind, some no longer knew the persons who came smiling and standing outside the windows.

With all of that in view, the words "pass away" came to be much more expressive of what happens at the end of life. Often, life's end is not so abrupt as it is gradual. A term like "pass away" describes a vanishing point on a horizon. It so describes what happens at the end of one's life. The steps away are so gradual with each frame of the moving picture changing just ever so slightly until there is a frame which seems just a dot before the oblivion as it vanishes from sight. And so one passes away.

If that were the end, then we would be, as the Apostle says, "of all men, most miserable."[58] But for the Christian there is hope. In this increasingly bleak time of gray and listless days,[59] there is no hope outside of the Christian

---

[58] 1 Corinthians 15:19 says: "If in this life only we have hope in Christ, we are of all men most miserable" (AV).

[59] "Stress Level of Americans Is Rising Rapidly In 2022...," The American Institute of Stress, Accessed June 7, 2022, https://www.stress.org /stress-level-of-americans-is-rising-rapidly-in-2022-new-study-finds. The opening lines of the article report (see next page):

faith. There it is. I have said it. I believe it with all of my being. What, then, is the hope of the Christian? What rescues us from that dreaded end of simply and wholly passing away into a vanishing point of oblivion?

Jesus. There are no more wonderful words than the ones which He uttered just as His own disciples were beginning to be persuaded to understand that Jesus was leaving them. He was returning to the Glory He had enjoyed eternally at the Father's right hand. The path of that return was rising up before Him, and it would be gruesome and horrific as He was beaten and as He was nailed to the cross.[60]

And why was it to be? Why did He submit to such an awful eternal plan of redemption? The short answer is that in doing so, He would fulfill the pictures and promises set forth through the Jewish sacrificial system involving blood being shed to cover and to atone for human sin.[61] It was the way that the Triune God had

---

Breaking it down, the **Stress in America Survey 2022** offers the following insights: 81% of Americans who participated in the poll were stressed out due to Supply Chain issues; 87% Americans are stressed due to the rising inflation in the country, up from 59% in August 2021 and 58% in June 2021. 80% Americans are tensed and stressed about possible Russian cyberattacks or nuclear threats to the US; 69% Americans fear that a World War III could break out and we are in the genesis phase of it; and 65% of Americans responded that they were stressed about money and the economy.

[60] Matt. 16:21.

[61] Hebrews 10:4 stated: "For it is impossible for the blood of bulls and goats to take away sins" (NASB). The author of Hebrews further explains that only the blood of Christ could cleanse us and fit us for eternal life with the righteous and Holy God (Heb. 10:11–14, 10:22–23).

designed to present His plan of eternal redemption to humankind, and Jesus did not shrink from fulfilling the words of the prophets from the Old Testament: words that predicted the sufferings of the Messiah—that special One sent by the One, True God. He did not shrink from it because those sufferings and that death were what made up for human sin. He was doing all of this to take our place. He was dying the death that sin deserves, though He, Himself, had no sin.

As Jesus' disciples began to comprehend the reality of His imminent death, He comforted them with the sweetest of words in our Gospel of John.

> "Let not your hearts be troubled. Believe in God; believe also in me. In my Father's house are many rooms. If it were not so, would I have told you that I go to prepare a place for you? And if I go and prepare a place for you, I will come again and will take you to myself, that where I am you may be also. And you know the way to where I am going." Thomas said to him, "Lord, we do not know where you are going. How can we know the way?" Jesus said to him, "I am the way, and the truth, and the life. No one comes to the Father except through me."[62]

---

[62] John 14:1–6 (ESV).

Chapter Nineteen

"Snakes in the Basement"

It may have been the fall of 2005, and I was at Lowe's trying to figure out how to make a wood stove work. My wife is an inveterate garage-saler, and one Saturday she found a wood stove for a good price. She bought it. I went and picked it up (well, wiggled it back and forth up the ramp and onto my trailer). It weighed about 250 pounds. When I got it home, I hooked up chains to it and used my tractor loader to remove it from the trailer. I then set it on the step just outside the door to the barn we were redoing as our home. I wiggled it some more and got it inside, but then what was I to do with it?

To say that I am not handy is something of a truism. (It's like saying the sky is down—if you live in Australia!) So that's how I got to Lowe's on the following Monday morning. While I was there, I bumped into two contractors I knew from church. When I saw the first one,

I told him I was needing to put in a stove pipe for the new wood stove. He said to cut a hole in the wall and stick the pipe together. He had done it numerous times when he lived in Alaska. "No big deal." The other one said I needed a large 25-foot-high masonry, chimney type structure: "Oh, probably about two grand." I didn't have two grand!

I wandered over to the how-to books. There wasn't a book on the topic of stove pipes and wood stoves. And then John Robinson bumped into me. Really! Literally. By this time John and Leslie had been coming to Maplewood Church for about five years, and it was ten years before they lost their health.

"Oh, excuse me, Pastor Eddie!"

"Well, hi, John!"

"What are you doing here, Pastor Eddie?" [Since you already know the answer to that question, I kindly will not be persuaded to repeat it.] John was the son of a blacksmith. He had retired as a fire marshal from the Air Force. His second career was welding.

John then said words I will never forget. "Well, would you like for me to help you?"

"Oh, wow, would you, John?" And so he did.

We went to the stove pipe part of the store. I didn't know the diameter of the opening at the top of the stove, so there was nothing else we could do until we drove 12 miles to my farm to look at the stove. John examined it. He said it was missing a piece—a connective piece—some sort of metal collar that clamps the stove pipe onto the top of the stove.

The most intelligent utterance I could conceive was: "Ohhhh!"

John and I drove all over town to other hardware and home improvement stores, and we could not find one anywhere. Finally, about 4:00 that afternoon he said, "Well, would you like for me to make you one?"

"Oh, wow, could you, John?"

You would just have to have known John Robinson to comprehend this. He turned his head sideways with a mock frustrated look that said, "Well of course I can make it. I can do anything." And he could.

A few days passed, and John brought the metal collar to my house. The collar was two inches high and fit the circumference of the stove pipe. He had bent the quarter-inch thick metal into a perfect circle, and the very ends of the piece of steel were perpendicular to the ends of the circular collar.

Through those perpendicular pieces he drilled a hole for a quarter-inch bolt to pull together the ends of the clamp when the nut was tightened. He painted it black like the stove. It was perfect because it was made by a professional. John put the collar clamp on the lower piece of stove pipe. He then asked, "So, Pastor Eddie: how are you going to attach the stove pipe to the outside of your barn?"

My barn was 25 feet high at the peak, and I had given this some thought. Before I became an English major who was unable to find work, I had thought about being an engineer, because my uncle had made a lot of money being an engineer.

I described my elaborate one-inch pipe system with elbows and t-joints and one-foot-long sections of pipe and the round, flat piece with threads in the center and with four screw holes in it so it could be attached to the side of the barn. I would make a square out of footlong pieces of pipe, and I would fit them together with t-joints and elbows. Next, I planned to use one-foot straight pipes and t-joints to attach the one-foot square of pipes to the barn. That would make it one foot away from the barn, and it would hold the 10-inch, double wall stovepipe in place.

It was rather ingenious, and John said, "Wow, Pastor Eddie. That's a really good idea. How much did you pay for the pipe?"

"Oh, about $165."

He shrugged a bit and proffered, "I could make something for free."

"Oh, wow, could you, John?" And he gave me that look; I saw that look numerous times.

A few days later he brought to my barn some aluminum straps. He brought the tank from an old hot water heater—a steel tank about five feet tall. He had cut a hole in the lowest part of the tank so that I could clean out the tank after I brushed out the stove pipe. He made a metal plate to cover the clean out port. The tank he placed under the 21-foot-tall stove pipe and cap to hold the weight of it. (He had, of course, asked me at one point how I was going to support the weight of 21 feet of pipe and cap.) The aluminum straps would be attached to the barn to hold the pipe in place.

Then he asked me how much I paid for the triple-wall insulated stovepipe to go through the wall. If one was recommended, I wanted two of them to reduce the heat near the wall. "I paid $100 for each of them—$200."

"You know I have one of those at home that I would give to you for free. And what were you going to put on top of the stove pipe?"

"Well, they made this piece—this cap." I knew the question he was about to ask, but I waited.

"How much did you pay for that?"

"That was $120." I knew what he was about to say, and you now know as well.

"I could you make you one of those for free." And he did. And then he took the 6 three-foot sections of ten-inch, double-walled stove pipe to his workshop. The area between the two walls he stuffed full of fiber-glass insulation he had saved from another project. One day he and another friend helped me set the 21-foot stovepipe on top of the five-foot-tall hot water heater tank. (When I say they "helped me," the reader understands exactly what I mean.)

"Now, Pastor Eddie. This is the most important job today. Someone has to stand over here to make sure the stove pipe looks straight when we put it up."

"But I wanted to help!"

"I know you did, Pastor Eddie, and this will be a big help. Believe me—this will help A LOT!"

There were times when I had problems getting used to heating with wood. If the wood stove wasn't drafting as it should, John would come over and troubleshoot. He liked to come out to my farm, and I enjoyed our visits. We talked about the Air Force, Alaska, his blacksmith father, his wife's mathematical knack for doing complex calculations in her head, the stock market, things which concerned him, and various biblical topics. One day he said he had something for me. He gave me the gift of a sharp ax and a sharpening stone. I treasure it. It's from my friend, John. He was one of the most remarkable men I have ever known.

Eleven years ago when I had surgery for melanoma, I planned my funeral—just in case I didn't last 11 more years or so. I contacted my dearest pastor friend—ten years older than I. I told Ken Sheppard that I had always wanted him to do my funeral, and then I said to him, "But now, you know, as I think about it, Ken, I think I would rather do *your* funeral!"

And there were songs and the various speakers and the order of the service and the pallbearers. I picked John to be one of my pallbearers.

One morning John called me and said, "Pastor Eddie, I need your help."

"Anything you ask me I will do for you," I immediately said.

"Come get the snakes out of my basement."[63]

I went over the next day with a flashlight, a bucket in which to put the snakes, and a pair of leather gloves. Sometimes snakes don't like to be grabbed, and some of their bites can be nasty! We went down into his basement. It was quite full. For a few moments I thought about clearing out my own storage area and throwing away all the things I have forgotten I have and thus would not miss. I have since repented.

---

[63] This account will give support for the fantasies of some who think that people who believe in the Bible also handle snakes.

He pointed to where he had seen the snakes. As soon as I got near that spot, sure enough, I saw a snake pull back its head. It disappeared. It looked like a black rat snake, a terribly common Missouri snake. I moved a box, and there he was. I grabbed him and put him in the bucket and slapped the lid on. The next one was harder to find, but I moved boxes around, and it slithered into another area. This one looked different—a duller color. (It was an eastern yellow-bellied racer—bluish, but with a green tinge linking the cream-colored belly to the bluish scales.) He thought he was successfully hidden, but I could reach in and grab him even though I could not tell what part of him I was grabbing. Into the bucket with the other one. Two snakes were in the bucket. One was about forty-two inches long, and the other one was forty-eight inches. John was sure there were more, but I could not find them, and I was late for an appointment. I brought them out to Brown Acres and released them in an area where mice and mouse runs were common. That should keep them busy and happy. I usually take photos of snakes that I catch, but I forgot to do so on this occasion.

Three weeks passed. John called, and he was a little bit frantic. "Pastor Eddie, you have got to come help me!"

"I'll always do anything you ask me to do." This time he said there was a snake upstairs—in the den—behind a flower planter. I have to confess I was a little dubious. Cracks in the wall and snakes going down to the basement, that's one thing, but snakes upstairs in November? "Okay, John. I'll be right there. Do you have some gloves for me?"

"I'll have them ready, Pastor Eddie."

I walked into the den. Was it a "snake den"? Sure enough, behind the planter, there was, indeed, some wide and scaly-looking thing. It was a cloudy November day, and I couldn't see it very well. But . . . it was on a table three feet off the floor. I moved the pot. I reached back in there with my hand. This time I took a picture. When you're scared to death of snakes, you're also scared of things that look like snakes. And, of course, it's a little hard to tell from across the room. In addition to this, John had very poor eyesight.

I took the picture, and I told John I was going to share his story. John Robinson had done so many things for me that I would do anything for him. I would even catch ratchet straps.

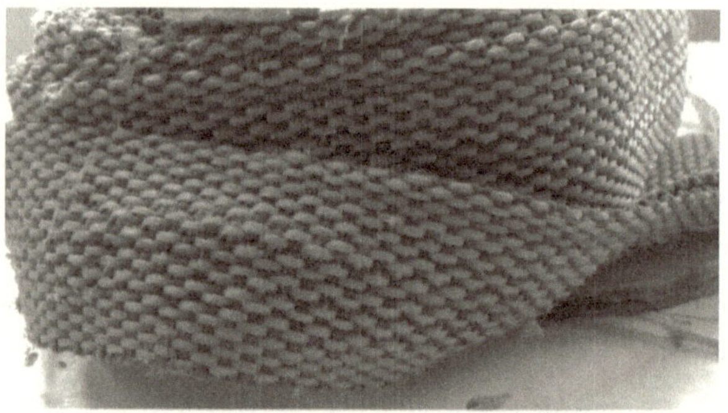

Chapter Twenty

"We've Got So Many Ways You're Bound to Like Some of Them."

I had been in Sedalia at Maplewood Church for a few years, and I was beginning to get to know the leadership of the church. They were an impressive lot. I found among them those who could have been leaders in large churches in large cities. They were that caliber of individuals. There was wisdom and life experience and faith.

And one of them was just a unique and fun person with whom I enjoyed spending time. Every conversation ended with the words: "Come see us." And we often did. No one ever made us feel as welcome as J.P. Sumner. Sometimes they would invite us; sometimes we would invite ourselves!

The kids enjoyed going to the Sumners' home—to the home of Norma and J.P., as we came to call him. His name was James Preston Sumner, and he introduced himself as "Jim Sumner." James Preston Sumner counted among his kin the infamous James brothers. His mother's maiden name was James.

J.P. often told the story that was told to him by his family. One day a group of riders on fine horses rode onto the farm of his grandparents. They asked if they could stay the night. They spent the night in the barn. The next morning as they were riding away, they said, "We might be kin." It was the James Gang of Jesse and Frank James. They had left behind a few pieces of gold.

Norma once told me that I am the one who started calling him J.P. We enjoyed their company as well as the company of Don and Brenda Eckhoff, whom they also had over for games like the domino game of Mexican Train. We seemed to sit in the same order for all of the game nights, but wherever we sat, Don always said at the conclusion of the turn of the person who played before J.P., "Your turn, James." J.P. would enjoy the banter that happened around any game, and he was never quick enough to play when his turn came around, at least as far as Don was concerned.

Many times I was there to play or observe a game of Rook with J.P. I concluded that it really didn't matter what he had in his hand. He would bid whatever it took to get the widow in the game. The total number of points one could make in the standard game was 120, but one variation in the rules of the game allowed a total of 130 points with ten points going to the one who took the last hand. I saw J.P. bid awfully close to 130 points many times. J.P. was a risk-taker, and he had fun whether he won or lost. If he lost, I could expect to see him shake his head back and forth and say that it was "just a silly kid's game."

On too few occasions J.P. and Norma invited us to go with them to their hometown, Lebanon, Missouri. Wes and I met them at their house, and we left early after we got the kids off to school. Norma had prepared coffee and sandwiches for us to enjoy as we drove down roads familiar and dear to J.P. There was never a moment with them that was awkward with silence. Conversations always flowed and were always interesting. There were serious times, and there were times that were full of fun. J.P. was an equal-opportunity teaser, and Norma would frequently shake her head and smile and say "James!" J.P. made people smile. And laugh!

Many times I would be standing with a group of men at church when I saw J.P. approaching. I then would see every head turn and every face smile in anticipation.

On one of our trips with them we went to the home in which he had grown up. We walked around the outside of the house and buildings. Not long after that outing, the land sold. I believe the hospital in Lebanon and a highway interchange gobbled up his old homeplace.

J.P. loved to tell stories of the past, and I heard many of them several times. One of those that I heard more than once was of his time in the Army and the huge mountain-of-a-man sergeant who could never get his name right. The sergeant would yell out: "Summers." There was that time in high school when he and another student raced school buses around the track that was on the outside of the football field in Lebanon.

I heard about the time one night he was going a bit over the speed limit when he met a highway patrolman on the familiar road north of Lebanon. He saw the trooper turn around. He knew the highway better than the officer, so at one point he topped a hill and turned quickly down a road to the right, turned off the lights, and coasted to a stop. It worked. He may have been in his ember glow Pony-Edition, hardtop Mustang then. To keep it in the family, that was the car he sold to his older son, Steve. When I once repeated the story in his company and in the company of others, he sort of wagged his head back and forth and said in a mock scolding manner: "You don't have to tell everything you know." I heard that phrase with some frequency, too!

He told about the time in his youth when he and friends were on a campout by the river. They were fishing at night, and they steered the old johnboat under a willow tree on the bank. They heard a thud, and when the flashlight shone on the source of the noise, it was a fat, wriggling cottonmouth. J.P. was equal to the threat. He picked up his trusty 12-gauge and BLAM! Right in the bottom of the boat. He got that snake!

Around the time we arrived in Sedalia, J.P. retired from selling insurance. He was fifty-six years old, and he could still sell insurance as the opportunity came up, and it often did. I went on a few sales calls with him. Retirement opened up the possibility for more travel for him and Norma. Sometimes they drove, and sometimes they flew to a distant destination and got a rental car. When he got back, we would always hear about the make and model of the car as well as the gas mileage and the price of gas where they had traveled.

Often the trip would be to some magical place called Seguin, Texas. At least, J.P. would enter into a reverie when he spoke of it. To me, it sounded like a dry and dusty place with cacti in abundance along with the occasional mountain lion. On balance, he spoke of the Texas bluebonnets and the Indian paintbrush, but my own remembrance of living in Texas was the summer heat and aridity. J.P. had relatives there: three nieces and two nephews.

As I mentioned, J.P. would very frequently say, "Come see us." When they were about to go on a trip, he would say, "You'd better come go with us." It was just that sort of statement that made me want to show up on the morning of the trip with my suitcase in hand, "ready to come go with them." I never did, but the trip would have been fun.

J.P. was the guy you never wanted to have sitting behind you. He would pull your shirt tail out of your pants, or he would tickle your side. He enjoyed gag gifts and odd conversation pieces like the battery-operated "Big Mouth Billy Bass Motion-Activated Singing Sensation Fish." He was the guy who would say, "What's that on your shirt?" As you looked down, he would flick his finger under your chin. The kind of jokes you expected from him were corny jokes, but you expected them to the point of asking for them, and you were never disappointed. My mother would retell one he told her: "What's the difference in broccoli and boogers?" The answer: "Kids'll eat boogers."

On a number of occasions, J.P. and I had gone together to follow up with visitors to church. On one occasion, there was a real openness in the couple to hear about how they could know that they knew Jesus as Lord and Savior. I shared with them from the Bible about God's unimaginable love and His plan to save sinners through the sacrifice and death of His son, Jesus. There was still a hesitancy as they continued to think about what they had heard—about how Jesus had died to save us from our sins.

Finally, J.P. asked the perfect question: "If you were to ask Jesus to save you from your sins, WHY would you do it?"

The reasonable response was immediate: "Well, so I wouldn't go to hell!"

"Then why won't you ask Him to save you?"

On those Sundays in church when J.P. would be in charge of calling the meeting to order and offering the opening prayer, he would often say something similar to this: "Welcome to Maplewood Church here on the north edge of the Ozarks. We've got so many ways you're bound to like some of them." And then he would often shake his head in that familiar way and say, "Pastor Eddie, . . . he's all right in some ways."

In his retirement he was able to be a regular on the opening day of trout season at his beloved Bennett Springs. I witnessed opening day only once, but it was a sight to behold. The fishermen were so thick in the water that they were unable to do the sashay-the-line-back-and-forth cast like you do with that type of equipment. I'm not making this up: there were places where fishermen were no more than six feet from the next fishermen. There were so many fishermen that the fisherman to fish ratio was three to one at best. A love of trout fishing was something that he passed on to his older son, Steve.

Bob, my next-door neighbor, was en route to Kansas City one day. On the way, he kept seeing the same luminous green Lincoln Town Car going past him. He saw it several times in the eighty-mile trip to Independence, a suburb of Kansas City. It would fly past, but twenty minutes later, there it went again. J.P. was the driver of the Lincoln, and he must have stopped a few times on the way and had to make up for lost time.

When Bob got home, he told me he had met a man who was from his hometown of Lebanon. He had met J.P. Sumner at a Tractor Supply store in Independence. Bob told me that he had seen J.P. flash past him several times, and it was easy for me to imagine that Mr. J.P. Never-Met-A-Stranger Sumner had introduced himself to my neighbor there in the aisles of the store. It so happened that J.P.'s father had been the rural mail carrier that delivered the mail to my neighbor's family throughout his childhood, and Bob remembered the elder Mr. Sumner.

When I saw J.P., I commented that Bob told me he had met him. I teased J.P. about speeding past Bob several times that day. J.P. told me that he had gotten to the point of inviting Bob to church. J.P. asked him if he had a church home. My neighbor said that he lived near Maplewood Church and went there. Well, . . . he did live near Maplewood Church. He had to live near the church if he was my neighbor. But I had never seen him in church, and I would have remembered it. And J.P. would have also, because J.P. faithfully met each visitor to church and welcomed each one.

It was not many months later that Bob was hospitalized. I visited him in the local hospital, and the time seemed right to ask him if anyone had ever shown him from the Bible how he could know that he knew Jesus as Lord and Savior. He said no one had. I asked if he would mind if I did. He said he wouldn't mind. That night he called on Jesus to save him. That night he became a Christian. J.P. had had the initial conversation with him, and I was privileged to lead him to Christ. A few months later, I conducted Bob's funeral in nearby Marshall, Missouri. I was thankful to be able to tell his friends and family that Bob had come to know Jesus in his final months.

There came a time when J.P. needed to get a heart catheterization. I think by that time I had had eight of them, and they had become pretty routine to me. As I write, I have eight heart stents in the arteries around my heart. By the time I had my tenth catheterization, they were so routine that on the day I was to go to the hospital in Columbia, an hour away, Wes was sick with a bad cold. I did not want to be couped up in the car with her, so I called a few retired friends to try to find a ride to the hospital. No one was available. I packed my bag that morning, anticipating an overnight in the hospital if I needed another stent. It was such a routine procedure for me that I had not done any advance planning, like getting gas for the car.

One of our parishioners, Bill Jackson, once spoke at a men's breakfast at church. He spoke of generational differences. He and J.P. were about the same age, and I think both were born in 1933. Bill noted that our generation would usually *arrive* on time to appointments and important events. His generation would *leave* on time! I prided myself in always being on time. Bill's implication was that my generation did not leave on time and would speed to make up for it. He was right in my case.

On that morning when I was driving myself to Columbia for my eighth stent, I had not *left* on time. I was scurrying around trying to get ready to go, and I left late. The information screen in my car said that my "range" was 67 miles. I had no extra time to stop and get gas. I reasoned that it was just 60 miles to the hospital, and I could get gas on the way home.

For a generation, the site of the entry point for catheterizations had been through the groin. At some point cardiologists began to use the wrist as the entry point. After that medical advance, catheterizations had become almost as routine to me as they were to my cardiologist, Dr. Anthony Spaedy. I left late, but I arrived on time, breathless with my heart jumping out of my chest.

J.P. was having his procedure done by the same cardiologist, and I had gone to the hospital that morning to pray with him and his family before the procedure. Keith, their younger son, was there with Norma and me. At one point a nurse came in to get J.P. in order to take him for a chest X-ray. Keith, Norma, and I walked out of the room as he was walking away with the nurse. He was in the typical hospital gown, and he still had on his little brown shoes and black socks. I thought it was funny, and Keith was smiling, but Norma had a smile on her face and her head cocked to one side like she thought he looked adorable. I had just a moment when he was about twenty feet away. I said loudly and urgently, "J.P., your flap's down!" Immediately, with both hands he covered his bottom. Of course, his gown didn't have a flap, but he didn't know that. In my defense, he would have done the same thing to me!

On one occasion, for no reason, I was daydreaming and thought that if I was driving across the country with a few guys, it would be fun to go with Don Eckhoff and J.P. in the group. I always had a half-smile around J.P. Either he was up to something, or I was. When my dad died shortly after our move to Sedalia, I lamented that he had not been able to get to know two men I know he would have enjoyed: Don and J.P. Sumner.

J.P. made my children feel special. Of course he had six wonderful grandsons of his own, but there was a sense in which at Maplewood Church, he was everybody's grandpa.

One day things turned serious. On a Sunday morning, he had fallen at home and had suffered a stroke. Had he had the stroke and fallen, or had he fallen and had the stroke? Norma had to call for help. Things were never the same again. We all come to that point, and we all have those who have gone around the bend just ahead of us. I was born the year that J.P. graduated from high school—the year he raced school buses around the track at Lebanon High School. J.P. has gone around the bend just ahead of me.

J.P. and Norma

I have heard Norma quote something I said once in a sermon. Just as I did on that occasion, Norma points with her fingers downward to signify our lifetimes here on earth. She then points upward to signify heaven. She has quoted me as I spoke of the Lord: "He takes care of us here until He takes care of us there."

As I mentioned before, the Apostle Paul spoke for the Christian in these words: "For to me, to live is Christ and to die is gain."[64] Paul also referred to death as being absent from the body but of being present with the Lord. The Psalmist wrote of our eternal home as being in the house of the Lord, forever. He elaborated on that

---

[64] Phil. 1:21 (NASB).

wonderful situation at the Father's right hand, that there are pleasures forevermore.[65]

As I heard J.P. ask: "If you were to ask Jesus to save you from your sins, why would you do it?" Again, the logical answer is, "So that I won't go to hell." J.P. would then ask, "So why not ask Jesus to save you right now?"

---

[65] Pss. 23 and 16 (AV).

Chapter Twenty-One

"Three Weddings and a Funeral"

Not every wedding goes as planned. Some of them do not even go as well as the rehearsal.

One of my pastor friends told me of a wedding in which the martial music of Richard Wagner's "Lohengrin" was sounding as the bride and her father paraded down the aisle. Suddenly, the bride quickened her pace in the little Methodist church. When she reached and rounded the front pew, she rushed to the left, and the crowd thought she was trying to escape. There to the left of the stage and just off the sanctuary in full view of the guests was the women's powder room. The bride was emptying her guts in the toilet, and she had not had time to close the door behind her. She emerged somewhat relieved, though quite ashen, and she plighted her troth to her beloved. Her beloved may be excused for passing on the opportunity to kiss the new bride.

Another pastor friend told me of the time he was about to preach a funeral. It was, of course, a somber moment as he walked up on the stage in the presence of the bereaved. He had been planning to remove the nail that continually worked its way out of one of the boards in the old and squeaky wooden stage. He never thought about it until it was too late to do anything about it, so it was just pounded down with a hymn book only to work its way out again at inopportune moments. The recalcitrant nail had raised its head again, and the pastor was robed and dignified as he lightly made his way to his pulpit. He tripped on the nail, fell flat on his face, and exploded his dignity!

But that was not the worst moment in his pastoral life. Jerome was something of a large gentleman. I suppose in those days when I knew him, he outweighed me by some 100 pounds, and he was no taller than my five foot nine. One of his parishioners had died, and Brother Jerome was soon to preside over the memorial service and the interment.

On the day of the funeral the ground was soaked and saturated from continual rains over the course of the prior few days. The family, under the shelter of umbrellas, had made their way from the funeral director's limousine and had sat down in the chairs provided for the elderly members of the family and for the widow. All of the proceedings would be under the sturdy-framed tent that would house a small number of supportive family and friends. The casket was arranged opposite the chairs, and an artificial turf carpet was placed over the mud and over the graves of other family members gone on to glory. A large lay of flowers had been set atop the casket by the funeral director and his staff. The casket rested upon the straps of a hand-crank apparatus that was designed to lower it slowly into the concrete vault in the six-foot grave.

The preacher was touched by the gravity of the situation and by the grief of the family. He so wanted to console them and give them a word of encouragement as they said their goodbyes and as he prepared to pronounce the funereal benediction at the conclusion of his remarks:

> Earth to earth; ashes to ashes; dust to dust. It is our sorrow to commend his body to the ground, but it is our unspeakable joy to commend his spirit to the Living Lord Jesus Christ who was raised from the dead and is coming again.

Very generally, the carpets often are covering four to six grave markers that become invisible tripping hazards for preacher and parishioner. Storm clouds gathered and thunder shook the tent as Brother Jerome concluded the brief service. He moved from the head of the casket and delicately avoided stepping too near the feet of the grieving widow in the center of the seated mourners. And as he bent down to shake her hand and promise his prayers, he felt the earth . . . move . . . under his feet. The soft and soaked mud broke away in an avalanche, and the portly preacher slid down into the grave beneath the casket like an otter on a mudslide on the Chikaskia River.[66]

---

[66] The Chikaskia and the Salt Fork Rivers run close to Tonkawa, Oklahoma, the site of my first pastorate.

I had a wedding ceremony in which I lost my voice after I prayed for the couple with words to this effect: "And Lord, may we be ready to help them if they are in trouble." And after I said it, I thought of those words, "in trouble," and agonized at their suggestiveness in that particular wedding. In former days, that type of wedding had been called a "shotgun wedding." After I said those poignant words in the prayer—that they were "in trouble"—I choked. I gasped and coughed, and I could not speak. The proceedings halted. Water had to be fetched. When I partially regained my voice, I could not regain much of my composure. When the wedding was over, I must have been too shaken to drive because Wes was driving. I was in such a state of despair and distraction and total humiliation that I told her, "I just want to leave town."

I imagine that was the way that Jerome felt after he was ungracefully hoisted from the grave. After all, he couldn't climb out because of the slippery mud. Jesus was not the only one to be raised from the grave, but I shouldn't say that.

During one recent wedding late in the day and on the beach at Jacksonville, Florida, as I was waxing eloquent in my charge to the bride and the groom, a fight broke out behind me and to my right. Two women were yelling and cursing and pulling each other's hair! And I had to miss it because I was looking the wrong way.

On another occasion, a young man asked his grandmother if I might consent to perform his wedding at the Chapel at Annapolis. He had not been close to the pastor in the Virginia church of his parents, and he had visited his grandmother and Maplewood Church many times over the years. I was delighted to have the opportunity to minister to the young midshipman and his fiancée.

The chapel was spectacular, and on Saturdays, weddings were scheduled every half hour, as I recall. The chaplain issued the order that the wedding was to be no longer than 20 minutes, and one party was herded out while another was ushered in. That afternoon we toured the campus, and part of the tour was to see the crypt of John Paul Jones. As America's first naval hero, he was known to me largely by his famous words: "I have not yet begun to fight!" It was all I could do to self-edit that day and not work those words into the vows of the ceremony with their particular relevance to any young couple.

One of my most memorable weddings was my first one at Maplewood Church. The day of the wedding arrived, and the guests were beginning to gather.

In most weddings at Maplewood, the grooms and their groomsmen would dress in one of the classrooms down the hall from my office. At one point shortly before the wedding, I emerged from my office to see the groom scurrying down the hall with his frilly shirt untucked and unbuttoned. He was rushing to the church office to call his mother, whom he expected still to be at a local motel. The wedding was to start in less than 45 minutes. His home was about 20 minutes away. He was sending his mother to his home to retrieve the ring! He had forgotten the bride's ring, and his mother was rushing to get it. Ten minutes later, his shirt was buttoned and tucked as he rushed down the same hall to the same phone to call his same mother. Fortunately he was able to reach her at his home because he had just remembered that he had forgotten to bring the matching ties that his groomsmen were expected to don for the wedding. She answered the phone and found both ring and ties. She then was rushing on her way to the church.

The wedding couldn't begin without the mother of the groom or the ring of the bride. All the while the bride and her attendants were fussing about and dressing in another part of the church. I got word to them that there would be a slight delay.

And then it was 2:00 and time for the wedding to begin. Mary Boatright was playing the organ and was moving through her planned prelude and shuffling papers to begin the Wedding March. At 2:08, I tried to appear nonchalant as I slipped up the side aisle near the organ and asked her to play the musical prelude again. She gravely nodded that she would.

Just moments later the mother of the groom appeared with the long-awaited ring and matching ties. The groomsmen hurriedly tied Windsor knots, and the groom escorted his mother to her seat. He returned soon and was ready to walk behind the pastor in great pageantry to await his beloved on the stage.

But wait! One of the groomsmen was missing. At the last moment he felt the violent urge to attend to business that could not be postponed. It was only 2:20 by that time, so he was not rushed and was able to accomplish a satisfactory evacuation. As he emerged from the men's room, the procession moved quickly to the stage to take the pre-assigned places. The brother of the bride was a ghastly and ghostly shade of green with a decided look of distress. It was a pale foreshadowing of what was to come.

As the Wedding March began, the bride and her father started that stroll which she had been dreaming about and he had been dreading.

The bridesmaids were in place. The groom, like many grooms, was trying to smile, and the brother of the bride was trying not to faint. Across the stage another drama was unfolding—or upsurging. The father of the bride had recited the lines that custom had written . . . "Her mother and I," and he had shakily taken his seat on the front row beside the woman who was softly crying.

And then it happened! First, the gurgling sounds escaped from the bride's sister. She tried to stifle them. Then, like Vesuvius or even Mount St. Helens it exploded, the great three-foot projectile of a breakfast burrito and a hurried and harried lunch of Black Forest Ham with Provolone on Italian Herbs and Cheese bread! Out, out it came, and it was followed by an encore! The term "aftershock" would be perfectly appropriate for its effect.

The bride turned to offer her ministrations to her younger sister, but I snatched her back to attention as the knees of her brother buckled and the brother of the groom moved quickly to tousle and ruffle the hair of that pale, green, cross-eyed groomsman so as to distract him from the events on the other side of the stage. It worked. He survived. They were pronounced husband and wife. For years a faded spot on the carpet reminded me of the spectacular events that had taken place there that day.

One Sunday after church, J.P. Sumner approached me and told me that his grandson's wedding was coming up and they had just found out that the pastor who was scheduled to perform the wedding was not able to do so. "If Caleb asked you to do it, what would you think?"

"Tell me about it. Where is it?"

"Upstate New York."

I had never met Caleb's fiancée, but I had heard that she was from New York. Caleb's father, Keith, made the next contact and said that they wanted Wes to come to the wedding as well.

Caleb was a young man who had grown up at Maplewood Church, and my every interaction with him from his youth had been a delight. He was as pleasant a young man as I knew. Like my own children, he was ready to spread his wings and fly as soon as he had heard the solemn tones of "Pomp and Circumstance." With his classmates, he had thrown with one hand his tasseled mortarboard high in the air as he clutched his diploma in his other hand. He and a classmate had moved to Phoenix where Caleb's friend,[67] Kevin, was in college.

J.P. had told me that Caleb had met someone there and that they were attending a little Baptist church in the Phoenix area. The pastor there had counseled them and prepared them for marriage, and then, without warning, the pastor had taken another church on the West Coast. He was not able to conduct their ceremony since he was still getting settled in his new charge.

Arrangements were made, and Wes and I flew into Albany, New York, rented a car, and drove an hour north

---

[67] I was tempted to write "Caleb's cousin's cousin" in the place of "friend," and that would have been accurate.

to stay in a cabin near Lake George. That evening we went to a large house in a deer-infested, wooded area to join the family and the bridal party for the rehearsal and dinner. The rehearsal could not take place at the site of the wedding because the wedding was to be on the deck of an 80-foot, three-decked, wooden boat that would cruise for the afternoon on lovely Lake George.

Introductions were made, and there in the house were Caleb's two brothers, one sister-in-law, his parents and grandparents, as well as the parents and family of the charming Casey Sanderson. We enjoyed a meal together, and then we began to try to rehearse the wedding that would take place the next day.

The bride was nervous.

She was an accomplished young woman with an MBA and a high-powered job with the state of Arizona. She was confident, funny, and able to speak her mind and to be frank. Clearly, she was able to control most situations. Now that I know her well and love her dearly, I would say that she would be a good hospital administrator or Chairwoman of the Joint Chiefs. But that night she was bouncing around wide-eyed and jumpy, and I thought we should hide the sugar and the caffeine. I had never seen a bride as . . . well, I have already used the word "nervous," so perhaps I should switch to "incredibly alert." She was so alert I truly wondered how things would go the next day. Caleb seemed as unperturbed as usual, so I thought nothing must be terribly amiss.

October 11 arrived, and we left for the shore of the lake. As Wes and I drove, we passed so many gorgeous scarlet and flaming orange and sunflower yellow trees that we ceased to comment on them. There were puffy clouds and wisps of white in the brilliant blue sky, and the surface of the water bounced and peaked with gentle waves. The lake would be a glorious sight and satisfying enough if it were in the middle of Kansas, but it was nestled at the bottom of the gentle slopes of the Adirondack Mountains, and they were overflowing with a cascading abundance of the same grand colors we had found so astonishing.

All the guests had arrived, and the boat had shoved off into the deep azure. Near the edges of the water there were times when the calm reflection of the glorious foliage against the Autumn sky made as pretty a sight as I had ever seen.

The captain came to a prearranged spot, and there he stopped the boat. The guests were gathered, and the wedding party assembled. As I walked past the bride, Casey leaned towards me and issued just one command in three New York words: "Make it quick!" Slightly taken aback, I said that I would. I did.

They said that they would and that they did. "I will." "I do."

"And now, in the presence of God and these friends and family who are gathered joyfully to witness your promises to one another, I pronounce you husband and wife. What God has joined together, let no one put asunder. You may kiss the bride."

All done in a personal record eight minutes! The remainder of the afternoon was spent cruising on a lake in the midst of some of God's most glorious creation.

Not all of life is weddings and flowers. Some of life is funerals and flowers.

I had been in Iowa for less than two years when I received the sad news of the death of a friend back in Tonkawa. The family asked if I might be able to come back to conduct the funeral.

I arrived on the appointed day, and when I dropped by the funeral home, there was no one there but the director. We really had had only a few conversations over the years, but once people almost get over their discomfort at being in the presence of a pastor, they often say the most incautious and, quite often, odd things. Especially if they are funeral directors! The funeral director at the end of the day was also a businessman, so perhaps I should not have been too shocked that he would offer the complaint, "Business has just been so slow lately!"

I remember the well-known director in Sedalia who was trying to get the crowd to come in closer for the interment service. We had traveled to Kansas together in the hearse for the burial, and I had noted his quirks in the two hours we had together. Riding that frequently in a hearse may have some real effects on one's mind. The director said to someone in the large group of elderly women who were there to mourn their lost friend: "You, the blue-haired lady, come on in closer!" Several ladies scurried closer at his invitation.

In the days leading up to another funeral, a funeral director was cautioned and reprimanded by his superior for seeking to hurry along the scheduling of the burial by suggesting that the departed loved one was "turning green." Perhaps riding too often in a hearse causes one to lose one's filter.

I have to confess that I, too, have ridden with some frequency in a hearse.

My second cousin, Loo, by any accounting, was a character. She was born in 1913 to an entrepreneurial farmer, Luther Brown, who had come to Mississippi from Kentucky. He had two brothers. One strayed as far as Indianapolis and lived out his life in a small, quiet neighborhood there. The other, Alonzo Brown, rode a horse to Brandon, Mississippi, and bought 200 acres nine miles north of town. The entrepreneurial Luther bought an old plantation—the house and a large acreage of cotton fields—just a few miles from Alonzo.

Alonzo had one child—my father, born in 1923. Luther married Etheleen Henley and had six children— Lavinia, "Loo," being the most intriguing of them all.

After her mother died, she lived for a time with my grandparents and became like a big sister to my father, ten years her junior. That made her like an aunt to me.

When Loo blew into town from her home in Hammond, Louisiana, she would stay at one of her houses in Mississippi. She had a city house and a country house, both filled with antiques. She attended all of my graduations, my wedding, and even Anna's wedding in 2005. When she entered the church during Anna's wedding rehearsal, this 92-year-old woman made every head turn. She was once a striking beauty; she was Miss

Jackson in the Miss America competition in the early 1930s. She had a presence about her.

Loo was a traveler—burning up the highways in the southern states, but she also traveled abroad on her last trip around the age of 90. She and an old friend went on a cruise in Scandinavia.

One Christmas Eve she arrived late to my parents' home. My father had died just five months before, and Loo was my only relative we knew well on that side of the family. It was always an event to host her. But this Christmas Eve—I think she was 87—she was still smoldering when she arrived. Thirty minutes earlier some pompous policeman *who did not know who she was* gave her a speeding ticket!

That year she bought a new Buick, the luxury one, and one year later I noticed the odometer had raced past 30,000 miles.

She loved diamonds, properties, fine cars, silver serving sets, and china. There was a ring that reportedly was appraised at $50,000. She was being courted to leave a bequest to her college alma mater, and the college president hinted that he might name a building after her. Maybe she left them something; I don't know.

Loo was, I believe, worth some 4 or 5 million dollars at the end of her life. During this period she had a property that had appraised for $4,000,000. Fifteen years before her death, Exxon had wanted to lease two acres of that land for $100,000 a year. She turned them down. She had consulted me for my opinion, but in the end, she didn't take my advice. After all, she was only 80 then and wanted to keep her options open.

In the last ten years of her life she bought a home near Brandon just seven miles from where she was born. By this time she had sold two of her other homes and her two rental houses. This home was something of a duplex—two separate living areas that shared a kitchen and a large living room. There was a nice guest house next to it. She bought this property with a gentleman friend, Eric, who had been her son's best friend growing up. When Loo's son, my cousin, Ralph, died at age fifteen, Eric became like a son to Loo.

Eric and Loo bought the house together, and he moved back home from Houston where he had retired from banking. Loo kept her main home in Louisiana, but when she came to Brandon to visit, she had her living quarters there in the duplex—a home away from home. What Loo and Eric had discussed was that he would pay the upkeep on the home. They each would pay half of the purchase price, and upon her death, the home would be Transferred on Death to Eric. Somehow, that's not what Loo put in the contract. It did, on the other hand, stipulate that Eric would pay the upkeep.

Loo called me on a Saturday to tell me she had cancer and that she was having surgery the following week. I was in the parking lot of a grocery store when I got the call. We talked about it, and then I asked her if she would mind if I showed her from the Bible how she could know that she knew Jesus as Lord and Savior. We had had some talks a few years before my own mother died, and now it seemed that Loo was near death. That evening, as I sat in the parking lot talking to Loo over the phone, she prayed with me to receive Christ. I left after church the next day for Louisiana so that I could visit her after her surgery.

The surgery was successful, and Loo lived another three years at least. One day I got a call from Eric. This time it was certain that she was near death, and he had just looked at their contract and found out that *Loo had not put in the TOD provision.* Eric asked, "Eddie, will you talk to Loo and ask her to do that before she dies?"

I talked to her, and she called a lawyer to her bedside a few days before her death.

I took a week's vacation to go and conduct her funeral. At the visitation the night before, I met many of my relatives for the first time—second and third cousins from Hickman County, Kentucky. I saw a handful of others of whom I had vague recollections from my youth.

At the funeral service I was thankful to be able to announce to a somewhat stunned family that Loo had prayed with me to ask Jesus to save her from her sins. Only the Lord knows the reality of her profession of faith, but I took sincere comfort in her prayer with me some three years before she died.

From the funeral home to the cemetery was a long fifteen-mile ride. It involved a Brandon police escort, a highway patrol escort, and a Jackson police escort. I rode in the front of the hearse with the funeral director. I mentioned at the graveside that the 45 MPH funeral procession was the slowest trip that Loo had ever taken. They all laughed, knowing her *many* speeding tickets.

That night back at the duplex, Wes and I stayed in the guest house, and Loo's more immediate family stayed in the main house. I learned that many of the closer family members already had a lawyer. It seems that Loo had made the change Eric had requested but had also rewritten her will so that she cut one close family member out of the will entirely. To the chagrin of the family, Loo had left the bulk of her estate to someone none of the family even knew! She seemed to have left her estate to someone who had been kind to her after her husband died. At least she didn't leave her wealth to a cat!

There was also one source of intrigue. No one knew where her $50,000 diamond ring was. But I thought I knew. Her eyes were closed, of course, but I had noticed a slight smile on her face there in the casket. I think the ring was clutched tightly in her right hand.

My wife has observed that a life can be overviewed with a listing of the times one's name appears in the newspaper. There is the birth announcement, the brief account of the marriage, and finally, an obituary. Perhaps one's name appears in the Dean's List published in some papers, or, sadly, in the crime report. From those two lists perhaps we might find the names of those represented in the bumper stickers: "My kid can beat up your honor roll kid."

The sober reality is that life is short.

Benjamin Franklin wrote a letter to a Madame Brillon, and the letter has come to us as "The Ephemera." The *Concise Oxford English Dictionary* defines "ephemera" as "things that exist or are used or enjoyed for only a short time."[68] Franklin's letter included a section in which he was quoting the imagined philosophical meanderings from the mind of the fruit fly. As the fly considered life, he wrote of life's brevity. He consoled himself with the suggestion from a fly friend of his that his name would be long remembered:

> My Friends would comfort me with the Idea of a Name they say I shall leave behind me; and they tell me I have *lived long enough, to Nature and to Glory:* But what will Fame be to an *Ephemere* who no longer exists?[69]

For the last year and more, funeral services and memorial services have been conducted much as they were before the terrible virus. However, during the days and months of Pandemic, we all knew someone who succumbed to the virus. Because of the early bans on large gatherings of mourners, especially when we were so traumatized by what was yet unknown about the level of danger the virus presented, memorial services were often postponed. There were many who died who were mourned from afar. They are remembered by their loved ones and close friends, but so much emotional energy was spent in seeking to avoid the contagion that many others who had just a casual acquaintance with the deceased have all but forgotten the ones who are no longer among us.

---

[68] *Concise Oxford English Dictionary,* 11th ed. (Oxford: Oxford University Press, 2004), s.v. "ephemera."
[69] Benjamin Franklin, "The Ephemera: An Emblem of Human Life," Bartleby.com, Accessed July 7, 2022, https://www.bartleby.com/109/1.html.

I am voicing the sad truth that most of us are little remembered and soon forgotten. As informal proof I offer my own inability to name anyone in my father's line beyond my great-great-grandfather. Unless I am mistaken, my sons cannot remember the name of anyone in their lineage beyond their grandfather. Some who might chance to read these words will have just the vaguest memory and scant knowledge of the illustrious Benjamin Franklin.

The Scriptures speak much about the brevity of life. The great king, David, recognized the uncertainty and brevity of life and prayed these words.

> Blessed are You, O LORD . . . forever and ever. Yours, O LORD, is the greatness and the power and the glory and the victory and the majesty, indeed everything that is in the heavens and the earth; Yours is the dominion, O LORD, and You exalt Yourself as head over all. . . . You rule over all, and in Your hand is power and might; and it lies in Your hand to make great and to strengthen everyone. Now therefore, our God, we thank You, and praise Your glorious name. . . . For we are sojourners before You, and tenants, as all our fathers were; our days on the earth are like a shadow, . . .[70]

David means by these words that we are here on earth for just a brief time, like visitors in a foreign land—like travelers simply passing through.

In another place David wrote that "Man is like a mere breath; his days are like a passing shadow."[71] Notice, they

---

[70] 1 Chron. 29:10–13, 15, 20 (NASB).
[71] Ps. 144:4 (NASB).

are not even like a *shadow*, but a *passing shadow*. They are like the shadow of a man walking past—brief, transitory, ephemeral, and fleeting. Beyond that, David also says that life is like a "breath." The Hebrew word *hebel* suggests brevity like the appearance and disappearance of one's breath on a cool morning. It is expired, and quickly it dissipates.

All of this urges the importance of coming to know as Savior the One who has conquered death and has invited mortal beings like you and me to a life that begins and never ends. That life begins with a new birth when one calls out in faith to the Lord Jesus. John's Gospel provides these words of salvation: "For God so loved the world, that he gave his only Son, that whoever believes in him should not perish but have eternal life."[72]

---

[72] John 3:16 (ESV).

Chapter Twenty-Two

"Life in the Real World"

The title song on an Alan Jackson album was "Here in the Real World." Jackson croons about the sad reality that the boy doesn't always get the girl in the real world. That was the sum and substance of the song. In country music and in church life, life is not always ideal.

What happens when pastors make mistakes? I'm not talking about the pastor who "mistakenly" embezzles $10,000 from the church building fund and then "mistakenly" finds himself at a motel in a nearby town "in the arms of a woman other than his wife."[73]

---

[73] I couldn't pass up this opportunity to explain the reason I used this phrase. A preacher was speaking on Mother's Day and seeking to honor his own mother. Somewhere along the way he lost it—his way in the story. His punchline was supposed to be that he found himself in the arms of a woman who was not his wife. It was his mother, he meant to say, but when he blurted out the phrase "I found myself in the arms of a woman who was not my wife," he forgot the next part. All he could come up with was: "And for the life of me I cannot remember who she

I am not writing of the horrendously long list of pastors, male and female, who have failed morally and been ejected from the pastorate. There is also a horrendously long list of pastors who have failed morally and have not yet been found out. And then there is the list of pastors who were found out but were not ejected!

I often think of an old preacher joke. Two pastors were walking along a city street when they encountered two men who were sitting on the curb by the gutter and drinking from a brown paper bag. As the pastors pass by, their noses seem lifted a bit and turned away from the two homeless men. One of the men lying in the gutter said to the other: "There, but for the grace of God, go I."

I am conscious of the grace of God in my life. I am saddened by every moral failure that comes to light, but there have been so many that are so terribly egregious that they have become a cautionary tale to others—a virtual proverb. Again, I am conscious of the grace of God in my life, for there, but for the grace of God, go I.

What I mean by "mistakes" are the real instances of the honest-to-goodness failure of common sense that occurs when we say the wrong thing, or say the right thing in the wrong way, or speak rashly, or lose our temper inappropriately, or forget something terribly important. It might be something simple and unintended like going to the local high school where the Veterans Day Assembly was the year before and not going to the courthouse where the Congresswoman from Washington

---

was!" It was not a very effective Mother's Day memorial; the preacher's wife enjoyed it least of all.

was awaiting your invocation along with the other two hundred guests! Of course, I am not suggesting that any of those things ever happened to me. I am saying that *all* of those things happened to me—not the motel thing or the Mother's Day message gone wrong, just to be clear! Nor the embezzlement!

I am plagued by several things that I have said over the years. I blurted something out in an effort to be clever, and it didn't come out right. Instead, it became offensive and hurt someone's feelings. I cringe when I remember the smart thing I said after a couple of cell phones had gone off in the morning worship service. It was quite clever and drew laughter, but the second call was an emergency call. One pastor I know was famous for a moment of intemperance when he commanded a young mother to "take that crying baby out of here." Whether it was said exactly like that or not, that is the way it was remembered. Several times it was remembered that way and expressed to me!

I remember a Facebook post I made in response to a dear person's mistaken word choice, and there was no way to take it back once I had hit "post" and had forgotten it. I found out that my words had been hurtful. My apology was accepted, but I have not been able to forget the incident, and the dear person wronged may not have forgotten it either.

Sadly, pastors are made of the same flimsy stuff other humans are made of. The Apostle Peter could not have been proud of the discussion recorded by the Apostle Paul in Galatians, chapter 2. The Apostle Paul must have flinched when his comrade-in-arms, Luke, enshrined for all time the account of one particularly sharp disagreement Paul and Barnabas had. They were about to leave on their second missionary journey. The issue in dispute was whether or not to take along the young disciple who had let them down once before.[74]

Wes worked as a dental assistant for Dr. William Hanson of Dallas. Dr. Hanson was the church organist for the famed First Baptist Church of the same city. Dr. Wally Amos Criswell pastored there for some 45 years until he was Pastor Emeritus. One Saturday afternoon, Dr. Hanson had gone on a picnic with his family. Late in the afternoon he had gotten wide-eyed when he remembered the wedding at which he was to play. He rushed to the church in shorts, donned a choir robe, and seated himself at his customary place on the bench and at the keyboard of the massive pipe organ. Dr. Criswell had already "assumed the position" as he awaited the wedding party's grand entry. He looked to his left and nodded solemnly to Dr. Hanson: "Good to see you, Bill."

Although I never forgot a wedding or a funeral, there was a well-known, retired and elderly pastor in Sedalia who was known as the "marrying-pastor." Performing weddings had become his side hustle. One Saturday afternoon he arrived early for his 2:30 wedding at Liberty Park at the ornate bridge that was near an arch. The arch and the bridge provided a perfect backdrop for photos of the bride and groom. While he was early at 2:15 for his 2:30 wedding, he had forgotten his 2:00 wedding scheduled to take place at the same place. Fortunately,

---

[74] Acts 15:39 (NASB).

Dean and his bride—the 2:00 couple—were wed and beginning their honeymoon by the time that the 2:30 bridal party arrived.

Many times parishioners told me of significant and tragic life and death issues at the back door of the church as they were leaving after my Sunday morning message. For years I had a Day-Timer wallet, and I could jot down any reminders for myself when the parishioner shared the concern. When my Day-Timer was replaced by a cell phone, I learned not to take the cell phone into the pulpit with me. And then I had nothing to jog my frazzled memory.

I learned too late in ministry that I should ask for a reminder from people concerning important events. I once forgot a parishioner's grief at the loss of her mother, and another time I forgot the news that a dear friend had just found out that he had cancer. He lived at some distance, and I rarely saw him, but a few months passed before I happened to call. He mentioned his treatment regimen. I was appropriately dismayed, and the couple was kind and gracious in accepting my apology. I know these things are inexcusable, and yet I had to beg forgiveness humbly for both of these awful failures. And the saddest thing of all is that there may have been other such failures, but these are the ones of which I am aware. My feet are not just of clay but of crumbling clay.

Churches and the search committees which represent them are often reactive. In writing that, I mean that they are prone to search for someone who is strong in the area of the most glaring and irritating weakness of the pastor they are seeking to replace.

The kindest and dearest pastors have flaws, but gracious and wise parishioners overlook them as they consider their own failures and inadequacies. While I was in the interview process for my third and final pastorate, one of my friends from seminary, Ken Quick, published a helpful article in *Leadership Journal.* The article was entitled "Pastors and the Peter Principle" and reflected the observation of a business and leadership guru of the time. His thesis was that people are often promoted beyond their level of competence to the level of their incompetence.

Ken wrote in his article that pastors are frequently evaluated in at least these three areas: relations with people; preaching, teaching, and proclamation; and the ability to produce and make things happen, whether church growth or building programs. He observed, "Pastors may have great strengths in one of the three areas and be adequate to strong in another, but few are strong in all three. We generally know the names of the thrice strong."[75] I will add this observation: those pastors whose names are well-known across the fruited plains, from sea to shining sea—those pastors live in mortal danger of falling "into temptation and a snare and many senseless and harmful desires that plunge people into ruin and destruction."[76] All pastors, well-known or unknown, live in the same mortal danger!

In the pastorate, notoriety is both benefit and bane. The British journalist of yesteryear, Malcolm Muggeridge,

---

[75] Ken Quick, "Pastors and the Peter Principle," *Leadership: A Practical Journal For Church Leaders,* XI: 3, (Summer 1990): 101.
[76] 1 Tim. 6:9 (ESV).

wrote a book entitled *Christ and the Media*. As a media person himself, he knew the temptations that befall the celebrity. He said that if Christ had lived in our time, the fourth temptation of Christ would have been the temptation to appear on television.

One professor from Dallas Theological Seminary who marked his generation was Howard Hendricks. Over and over he warned us, "Don't believe your press reports." Charles Spurgeon said somewhere in his *Lectures to My Students* that "Those who praise us are probably as much mistaken as those who abuse us." Of Spurgeon's own temptation to pride, he further said that those with hearts easily kindled with the fires of pride must keep far away from themselves those who would kindle such unquenchable fires with praise. The modern pastor has to preach to himself the necessity of humility—often.

One of the dangers brought to us during the time of Pandemic is that churches closed or limited attendance to help to tamp down the spread of the virus which continues two years later to arise in its variants and mutations. Parishioners who stayed home during the Pandemic may have been exposed to media preachers who were better coiffed than their own drab and plain pastors who frequently appeared sans makeup. That local preacher may have snaked a backed-up church toilet and mopped up the overflow as he missed half an hour's time of preparation for the divine appointment that is the preaching event. He may also have been at the hospital past midnight the night before. The local pastor may suffer from comparison to the media personalities because he or she lacks researchers and assistants and publicists.

A final reason churches are still struggling these many months after the Pandemic is that some parishioners also came to enjoy not just breakfast or coffee with the sermon but also pajamas with the sermon.

Another real issue of life in the real world is that some pastors struggle with depression. One of my goals in writing this book was to offer encouragement in a difficult time, so I do not want to dwell on this subject, but the truth is that pastors suffer from depression and melancholy at virtually the same rate as the general population, I believe. Most people, at some point in their lives, will face a bout with extended discouragement or depression. I recorded these words in my journal on March 21, 1980. I had been in the pastoral ministry, at that time, for some eleven weeks.

> How is it that yesterday at this time I desired to move back to Mississippi and live on the farm? I was in a fearful fit of depression—fearful because I remember where I was a year ago and how sleep fled from me as the moon before the dawn. It was bleak and black, deep and dark, but time in prayer brought me around. And I must mention the one that God so often uses to encourage me—my wife. Thank you, Father, for a wonderful woman. I bask in your love and in hers. When I ask why I had a yesterday, perhaps it is in order that I may comfort those in need of comfort.

One Sunday morning I looked out in the congregation to see a pastor from another local church. That was not terribly unusual. A few others had visited our church when they happened to be in town and on a "stay-cation." A few others came to sit among us for a time, seeking to heal after a painful termination from their pastorates.[77]

As I visited with the dear brother after our service, I discovered that he had resigned abruptly from his church. He was in the throes of deep depression. We followed up that conversation with lunch the next day. A few other visits took place as his life fell further into the abyss. His wife left him, took their children, and went back to live with her parents. The depression was beyond the transitory blues that many experience. It was not just episodic but had been a struggle for many months. Within a month he left town, and I lost track of him.

It is very likely that the people who sat before him on Sunday mornings did not know that he was struggling for his very life. It may be that he was counseling one of his parishioners who also was walking on the edge of the cliff. Parishioners live their lives in the real world, but pastors do as well.

I was present once when a pastor was pouring out his heart to an older pastor. He was expressing his doubts over whether or not he could continue in ministry. I, also, certainly had my moments, and I can commiserate with

---

[77] Hershael York, a preaching professor at Southern Baptist Theological Seminary, reports the results of a study: "As many as four in ten pastors will be forced to leave a church—either by firing or pressured resignation—at least once during their ministry careers, according to researchers." See article "Pastoral termination common but oftern avoidable...," BaptistPress, Southern Baptist Convention, Accessed July 8, 2022, https://www.baptistpress.com/resource-library/news/pastoral-termination-common-but-oftern-avoidable-experts-say/. [The word "often" is spelled as it appeared.]

such sentiments. More than once in ministry I looked at my own church situation and wished I had gotten the pharmacy degree that I considered before I considered seminary. Many times, especially after decades of ministry, I felt as though I was trapped in the pastorate. I felt as if the Lord had me trapped! Life and ministry had become difficult, and like the Psalmist expressed: ". . . Oh that I had wings like a dove! For then would I fly away, and be at rest."[78]

One day a pastor friend called to chat about some of his struggles in ministry. As the conversation wore on, I heard him say that every day, the first thing that he read before his Bible was the want ads, half-heartedly looking for other employment. I then heard the words: "I read the obituaries with envy."

These words from this pastor reflect desperation. People in every profession and job have low moments as well, but somehow, we think of pastors as being above it all. We think that they are the ones that wade first into the Jordan to part the waters before the rest of us.[79] The reality is that pastors, like parishioners, have both triumphs and failures. Pastors and pedestals don't mix.

These sad tales are no way to end a book intended to offer refreshment for the weary, but as bad as they are, at least the following incident happened in my first church in Tonkawa *after* I had moved far, far away to northern Iowa.

---

78 Ps. 55:6 (AV).
79 Josh. 3:8–13.

When I was still at Tonkawa Bible Church, it eventually fell to me to clean the church building. Joe Marshall was too old to do it, despite his willing spirit. I wrested the broom from him and began to clean the building each week so he would not have to do it. I found that the time passed more quickly if I would listen to the radio or a sermon tape as I worked. There were speakers upstairs in the sanctuary and downstairs in the basement. The sound system controls were in the church office which was also the pastor's office. In the sound system was a turntable for wax records, a cassette tape player, and an AM/FM radio.

The cassette tape system could be used when we used an accompaniment tape for a children's Christmas program. *A knob had to be turned to switch between the record player, the tape player, and the radio.* And this is where the trouble comes in.

As I said, we had moved on to Iowa, and just seven months later, the solemn and expectant assembly of parishioners had gathered for the children's Christmas program. The tallest children played the roles of the shepherds, and others with more speaking parts played the roles of Mary and Joseph and the innkeeper. The smallest children were dressed as sheep and cows, and the remaining toddlers made up the squadron of angels with glitter, chiffon wings, and gold-wire-wrapped coat hangers forged into haloes.

The choir director went into the church office intending to turn on the cassette tape for the program. Unknown to her, the sound system had been switched to play the AM radio, probably while someone cleaned the church the day before.

As the children were prepared to sing "Silent Night" to the accompaniment tape, the sound system instead blared out at a startling volume the opening words of a familiar commercial of the day: "Attention, hemorrhoid sufferers!"

The assembly was no longer solemn!

My hope and prayer in writing this book has been that it might provide some diversion for a time—some solace and comfort for the lonely and fearful days in which we find ourselves.

I hope from time to time, as you read these words, that you smiled.

About the Author

Eddie Brown is a retired pastor living in mid-Missouri after serving three churches in the Plains and the Midwest over a period of 38 years. Eddie grew up in Brandon, Mississippi. While in college and working with Youth for Christ in Jackson, he met his future wife, Wesley Heard. They have three children and nine grandchildren.

At Mississippi College Eddie studied English Literature and Philosophy. He majored in Old Testament and Semitics at Dallas Theological Seminary and received his Doctor of Ministry degree from Covenant Theological Seminary.

In retirement Eddie enjoys speaking in area churches and pursuing his hobbies of reading, writing, mowing, planting trees, cutting firewood for their wood stove, and chauffeuring around the only three grandchildren who live nearby. He and Wes live on a hobby farm known as Brown Acres, and you can meet their six collies on Facebook via Brown Acres Collies.

In high school Eddie played on a state championship basketball team, and while he did not get a lot of playing time, he received the Sportsmanship award his senior year.

www.ingramcontent.com/pod-product-compliance
Lightning Source LLC
Chambersburg PA
CBHW020908160726
47993CB00005B/1866